THE EUROPEAN UNION AND CENTRAL AND EASTERN EUROPE

The European Union and Central and Eastern Europe
The implications of enlargement in stages

SUSAN SENIOR NELLO
University of Siena and Robert Schuman Centre, Florence

KAREN E. SMITH
London School of Economics and Political Science

LONDON AND NEW YORK

First published 1998 by Ashgate Publishing

Reissued 2018 by Routledge
2 Park Square, Milton Park, Abingdon, Oxon, OX14 4RN
52 Vanderbilt Avenue, New York, NY 10017

Routledge is an imprint of the Taylor & Francis Group, an informa business

Copyright © Susan Senior Nello and Karen E. Smith 1998

All rights reserved. No part of this book may be reprinted or reproduced or utilised in any form or by any electronic, mechanical, or other means, now known or hereafter invented, including photocopying and recording, or in any information storage or retrieval system, without permission in writing from the publishers.

Notice:
Product or corporate names may be trademarks or registered trademarks, and are used only for identification and explanation without intent to infringe.

Publisher's Note
The publisher has gone to great lengths to ensure the quality of this reprint but points out that some imperfections in the original copies may be apparent.

Disclaimer
The publisher has made every effort to trace copyright holders and welcomes correspondence from those they have been unable to contact.

A Library of Congress record exists under LC control number: 98072627

ISBN 13: 978-1-138-38728-7 (hbk)
ISBN 13: 978-1-138-38729-4 (pbk)
ISBN 13: 978-0-429-42635-3 (ebk)

Contents

List of Tables	vii
List of Figures	ix
Preface	x
Acknowledgements	xi

1 **Introduction: The Prospect of Eastward Enlargement of the EU in Stages**   1

2 **The EU's Membership Conditions: Assessing Fulfilment**   5

   The Economic Criteria for Enlargement   5
     Progress in creating a functioning market economy   5
     Capacity to cope with competitive pressures and market forces within the Community   12
     Adherence to the aim of Economic and Monetary Union   15
     Acceptance of the '*acquis communautaire*' concerning the Single Market   17

   The Political Criteria for Enlargement   19

3 **Consequences of Enlargement in Stages**   31

   Institutional Implications   31

   Implications for Budgetary Expenditures and Receipts   33
     Additional spending through the Structural Funds   34
     Additional spending on the CAP   37
     Expected contributions to the EU budget   39

   Economic Implications   39
     The impact of enlargement in stages on trade   39
     The impact of enlargement in stages on agricultural trade   42
     The possibility that firms remaining outside the EU lose their relative competitiveness   45

The impact of enlargement in stages on foreign direct investment in the CEECs	46
The impact of enlargement on growth	49
Possible implications of enlargement in stages for the location of industry	50
Labour migration	53
Implications for Security and Foreign Policy	55
4 Managing Enlargement in Stages	65
5 How to Grasp Diversity: Institutionalise It?	69
Appendix	73
Bibliography	109
Index	117

List of Tables

1	Main Features of the Europe Agreements	73
2	The Fiscal Criteria and Inflation in the CEECs	74
3	Interest Rates in Selected CEECs and EU Members	76
4	Exchange Rates of CEECs' Currencies	77
5	Changes in GDP, Investment and Unemployment in the CEECs	78
6	Indicators of the Macroeconomic Performance of the CEECs	79
7	The Structure of Production	80
8	Progress in Transition in the CEECs	81
9	The Share of Intra-industry Trade in EU Trade with the CEECs	83
10	Total Assistance from G-24 Countries to the CEECs, 1/1/1990-31/12/1995	84
11	G-24 Assistance Commitments	85
12	EBRD Indicators of the State of Democracy	86
13	Principles in the Convention for the Protection of National Minorities	87
14	Votes in the EU Council of Ministers	88
15	Balance of Power within the Council of Ministers	89
16	The Impact of Successive Enlargements on the Size of the Community	90
17	GDP Per Capita in the CEECs and Poorest EU Member States	91
18	Estimated Cost of Enlargement for the Structural Funds	92
19	The 1994-99 Financial Perspective	93
20	Extra CAP Spending per Year as a Result of CEEC Accession	94
21	Basic Data on Agriculture in the CEECs 1993	95
22	CEEC Share of Production of Various Agricultural Products in the Enlarged EU total (1994)*	96
23	Estimated Relative Contributions to the EU Budget	97
24	EU-CEEC Trade	99
25	The Increase in EU*-CEEC Trade over the 1989-95 Period	100

26	The Increase in the EU Share of the Total Trade of Selected CEECs over the 1989-95 Period	101
27	Tariff Reduction Envisaged by the Europe Agreements as Modified by the Copenhagen Summit	102
28	Commodity Concentration in Exports to the EU	103
29	CEEC and Mediterranean Basin Market Shares of Total Extra-EU Imports of the EU(12)	105
30	CEEC-EU Trade in Agricultural Products	106
31	FDI Inflows to the CEECs	107

List of Figures

1	Inflation in Selected CEECs	75
2	The Possible Relative Weights of CEEC(10) Votes in the Council of Ministers on the Basis of Population	89
3	Proposed Spending from the EU Budget (1998)	93
4	Estimated Relative Contributions to the EU Budget	98
5	Net Foreign Direct Investment	108

Preface

This is a revised and enlarged version of a background paper first presented at the May 1997 meeting of the European University Institute Working Group on Eastern Enlargement, and published as a European University Institute working paper (RSC no. 97/51). Susan Senior Nello is responsible for the economic content of this book, and Karen Smith for the political and institutional aspects.

The authors would like to thank the members of the Working Group for their useful comments on the background paper. We would also like to thank Jan Zielonka and Yves Mény for involving us in the Working Group and encouraging us to undertake this research. A particular thanks is also due to Brigitte Schwab and Shirley Artis for helping us to prepare the final version of the text.

Susan Senior Nello and Karen E. Smith

Acknowledgements

The authors and publishers wish to thank the following for permission to reproduce copyright material:

Baldwin, R.E. (1994) Towards an Integrated Europe, CEPR, London, Table 7.13 on page 186 and Table 7.14 on page 187.

Baldwin, R.E., Forslid, R. and Haaland, J.I. (1996) "Investment Creation and Diversion in Europe', World Economy, vol. 19, no. 6, November, Figure 1, p. 640.

European Bank for Reconstruction and Development, Transition Report 1997, Table 2.1, pp. 11-13

European Economy, Reports and Studies, no 6, 1994 "The Economic Interpenetration between the European Community and Eastern Europe" Table p. 27 and table p. 163

UN/ECE Economic Survey of Europe in 1995-1996. Tables 3, 5, 6 p.114 and Tables 3, 6, 11 p.149

World Development Report 1996, Table 1 on pp. 188-189 and Table 12 on pp. 210-211

1 Introduction: The Prospect of Eastward Enlargement of the EU in Stages

Ten Central and East European countries (CEECs) applied for EU membership between 1994 and 1996: Bulgaria, the Czech Republic, Estonia, Hungary, Latvia, Lithuania, Poland, Romania, Slovakia, and Slovenia. All ten have signed association ("Europe") agreements with the EU.[1] All are participants in the EU's "pre-accession strategy", which is to help prepare them for eventual membership.[2] Enlargement is widely considered to be the way to spread stability, prosperity and security eastward, and has been agreed to by the Union for that end.

Enlargement will depend on whether the applicant state meets certain conditions, which were laid down in June 1993 by the Copenhagen European Council:

- the applicant state must have a functioning market economy with the capacity to cope with competitive pressures and market forces within the Community;

- the applicant state must have achieved stability of institutions guaranteeing democracy, the rule of law, human rights and respect for and protection of minorities;

- the applicant state must be able to take on the obligations of membership, including adherence to the aims of economic and monetary, and political union; and

- the EU must be able to absorb new members and maintain the momentum of integration.[3]

It also seems likely that the speed and progress of the accession negotiations will depend on success in implementing the provisions of the Europe Agreements, and on progress in adopting the *acquis communautaire*, including the programme for regulatory alignment with the Single European Market set out in the Commission's 1995 White Paper.[4]

Clearly, not all ten countries will accede to the EU at the same time, because they will not all meet the conditions at the same time. Enlargement will thus take place in "waves", to some countries before others. The process can be thought of as one of "concentric enlargement", but this seems to indicate that the countries most likely to join in the first wave are those geographically closer to the Union.[5] Instead, "enlargement in stages" will be used here. The term is preferred to concentric enlargement because it does not imply that the process will occur first to those countries geographically closer to the Union.

Key decisions on enlargement were taken in 1997. The Commission presented its opinions on all the applications in July 1997, following the conclusion of the intergovernmental conference at the June 1997 Amsterdam European Council. In its communication, Agenda 2000, it recommended that membership negotiations begin with the Czech Republic, Estonia, Hungary, Poland, and Slovenia.[6] Several member states disagreed with that recommendation; there has been considerable discussion over how many CEECs, and which ones, should join in the first stage. Agreement was eventually reached at the December 1997 Luxembourg European Council: negotiations on entry began with the Czech Republic, Estonia, Hungary, Poland and Slovenia (as well as Cyprus) in spring 1998, and an "accession process" was launched with all ten CEECs in March 1998. The "accession process" has entailed the conclusion of "accession partnerships" with each CEEC, and additional pre-accession aid. The decision on beginning membership negotiations could, however, be amended prior to the first Eastern enlargement, if additional CEECs are considered ready for membership. The enlargement issue will therefore remain on the table for several years.

The approach used here is intended to be positive rather than normative (though in practice distinction between the two is sometimes difficult). In other words the aim is not to address the question of how, when and with whom should enlargement proceed. Instead, Chapter 2 attempts to identify criteria which could be used to decide whether countries are ready to join. Chapter 3 is concerned with the probable consequences of enlargement proceeding in stages. In particular, the aim is to assess whether (temporary) exclusion from the EU is likely to worsen the economic and political situation of the countries left out. The final two chapters will discuss possible solutions to the problems posed by enlargement in stages.

Notes

1. The main features of the Europe Agreements are set out in Table 1 of the appendix.
2. The pre-accession strategy was approved by the December 1994 Essen European Council, and includes PHARE aid targeted to helping the associates prepare for accession, and the structured relationship, in which the associates and the various sectoral, and General Affairs, Councils meet regularly. Péter Balázs charges that the EU's treatment of the Central and East European associates is thus increasingly uniform, without differentiating between faster and slower reformers. Balázs (1997), pp. 11-12.
3. European Council in Copenhagen, 21-22 June 1993, Conclusions of the Presidency, SN 180/93, p. 13.
4. EC Commission (1995b).
5. The term derives from "concentric circles", the design for the post-Cold War European architecture advocated in 1989-1990 by Commission President Jacques Delors and German Foreign Minister Hans-Dietrich Genscher. The Community, at the centre, would be strongly integrated, and surrounded by countries that were more closely linked to the Community the closer they were geographically to it. Tight links would be established with the EFTA countries, via the European Economic Area, whereas the East European countries would become associates. The Community would maintain looser ties with the Soviet Union and other outsiders such as the US.
6. Membership negotiations are also to begin with Cyprus, whereas Malta, another prospective membership candidate, has suspended its application. EC Commission (1997).

2 The EU's Membership Conditions: Assessing Fulfilment

The economic criteria for enlargement

In order to consider the economic conditions for membership, the next section will discuss the indicators which could be used to assess the extent to which the CEECs have developed "functioning market economies". The section which follows will deal with the capacity of the CEECs to cope with competitive pressures and market forces within the Community. Then there will be a brief description of what is implied by endorsing the EU objective of economic and monetary union, before considering what is implied by acceptance of the *acquis communautaire* in the area of the Single Market.

To date the Commission has failed to assign weights reflecting the relative importance of the different criteria. As the range of criteria is so wide, and some of these may be in contradiction with each other, the EU has a certain amount of discretion in deciding which applicant countries should join when. However, since the publication of Agenda 2000 and the opinions on the applicant countries, a clearer picture of how the Commission is intepreting the criteria is beginning to emerge.

Progress in creating a functioning market economy

In assessing the extent to which the CEECs have developed functioning market-oriented economies, Agenda 2000 lists a number of conditions which should be met[1]:

- equilibrium between demand and supply is established between the free interplay of market forces, and prices and trade are liberalised;

- there are no significant barriers to market entry or exit;

- the legal system is in place;
- there is broad consensus about the aims of economic policy; and
- the financial sector is sufficiently well developed.

In order to see how far these conditions are realised in the applicant countries, account has to be taken of both their macroeconomic performance, and their success in microeconomic transition (restructuring and privatisation) and systemic change.

INDICATORS OF MACROECONOMIC PERFORMANCE

One of the risks in assessing the macroeconomic performance of the applicant countries is that too much importance might be attached to the ability of the CEECs to meet the Maastricht convergence criteria.[2] Though the requirement that applicant countries endorse the ultimate objective of EMU means that the CEECs cannot completely ignore the Maastricht criteria, it is essential to bear in mind that convergence criteria are not the same as accession criteria. Accession criteria should assess whether the applicant country has taken all the necessary political and economic reforms to prepare for membership. The Maastricht convergence criteria were introduced in an attempt to ensure that the constraints on policy implied by the EMU are acceptable to the country concerned. Their aim is to avoid destabilising the EMU by the premature admission of countries whose underlying economic performance is not yet compatible with permanently fixed exchange rates.

The Maastricht Treaty spelt out five criteria:

- Successful candidates must have inflation rates no more than 1.5% above the average of the three countries with the lowest inflation rate in the Community.
- Long-term interest rates should be no more that 2% above the average of that of the three lowest inflation countries. This is to ensure that inflation convergence is lasting, because otherwise higher expected future inflation in a country would be reflected in higher long-term interest rates.

- The exchange rate of the country should remain within the "normal" band of the exchange rate mechanism (ERM) without tension and without initiating depreciation for two years. At the time of the Maastricht Treaty the "normal" band referred to the margins of +/- 2.25%, but since August 1993, in some circles it is now taken to refer to +/-15%.
- The public debt of the country must be less than 60% of GDP.
- The national budget deficit must be less than 3% of GDP.

The last two on the list (iv and v) are referred to as the "fiscal" criteria and are subject to an escape clause. A country may be granted a waver if the gap between the actual and reference situation is "exceptional and temporary" or if the excess in public deficit or debt is declining "continuously and substantially".

There are several drawbacks in using the Maastricht criteria as indicators of the progress in economic transition of the CEECs:

- The Maastricht criteria are indicators of macroeconomic performance, and the experience of transitional economies suggests that in assessing their readiness to join the EU, account should also be taken of microeconomic developments (economic restructuring and privatisation), and progress in systemic change. Transition is an ongoing dynamic process and even if a CEEC meets the criteria at a particular moment, this is not necessarily a guarantee that it will continue to meet the criteria on a sustainable basis.[3]
- Even as indicators of macroeconomic performance the Maastricht criteria can be criticised. At times success in meeting the convergence criteria may be at the expense of foregone growth (or recession) and higher unemployment. Given the already high levels of unemployment in the CEECs, and the urgent need for economic restructuring, these further indicators ought to be taken into account.[4]
- Some of the concepts underlying the criteria (such as fiscal deficit or long-term interest rates) assume a different meaning in transitional and market-oriented economies.
- The priorities of macroeconomic stabilisation programmes as well as the difficulties which they encounter in the transitional economies may differ from those of existing EU members.

At present the inflation appears the criterion posing most difficulties for the CEECs, in part because of "inertial" inflation (Andreff, 1997) arising from transformation-related factors. As shown in Table 2,[5] with the exception of the Czech Republic and Croatia, inflation remains in double figures in all the CEECs. Economic transformation may contribute to inflationary pressures in a number of ways: through price liberalisation, the ending of the CMEA[6] trading system (and the consequent increase in energy prices), devaluation and increased public spending on infrastructure and unemployment benefits, wage indexation, and, in some countries, servicing of the public debt. As a result there may be increased inflationary expectations and these could prove self-fulfilling. In many cases the centrally-planned economies were characterised by excess purchasing power in the hands of the population (monetary overhang) because of the shortages of goods. The effect of price liberalisation was to render this repressed inflation open (Nuti, 1986).

The high levels of interest rates in most CEECs reflect the need to reduce inflationary pressures. The underdeveloped long-term capital markets in many of the CEECs means that data on long-term bonds is generally not available for these countries. Table 3 (in the appendix) therefore sets out both long-term bond yield for some of the present EU members, and the Central Bank discount rate and lending rates for these countries[7] and some of the CEECs.

The Maastricht criteria refer to public debt, but the legacy from the past means that in general data for the CEECs refers to foreign debt. The burden of foreign debt in Poland and Bulgaria (see Table 2, in the appendix) was such that both these countries were forced to seek rescheduling.[8] It was largely fear of loss of confidence (which might have jeopardised the relatively high level of foreign direct investment) that prevented Hungary opting for a similar measure. Debt service payments accounted for more than 25% of budgetary expenditure in Hungary and Bulgaria, and 17% in Poland in 1995.[9] The debt service burden of these countries is worsened by high interest rates which are used to combat inflation.

The concept of public deficit in the Maastricht Treaty refers to central, regional and local government as well as social security funds. As Daviddi and Ilzkovitz (1996) point out, the budget situation of local and regional governments is often difficult to assess in the CEECs. A clearer understanding of how privatisation has been taken into account in calculating public deficits is also necessary. The creation of adequate social safety nets is a central element of the transformation process and this could lead to a substantial increase in government deficits.[10]

Fiscal deficits are too high in certain CEECs (and notably Bulgaria) and external discipline and "borrowed credibility"[11] could play a useful role. However, as Tanzi explains (1993), there are various ways in which too much concern for budgetary constraint might hinder transition. For example, if state enterprises lay off workers, government spending on unemployment benefits is likely to rise. To avoid this increase in spending, governments might encourage firms to continue hoarding workers, and this could render restructuring and privatisation more difficult. If a country devalues its exchange rate, its interest payments on foreign debt measured in domestic currency will rise, adding to government expenditure. If the foreign debt is large, a rigid limit on the budget deficit might cause the government to delay exchange rate adjustment.

Also on the revenue side there may be a trade off between excessive concern for fiscal discipline and progress in transition. Transition entails reform of the fiscal system by introducing taxes on income and value added in place of turnover taxes, and by widening the tax base. The growth of a new, green-field private sector (sometimes refered to as "organic" privatisation) was accompanied by widescale tax evasion. Attempts to crack down on evasion could force many of these small new firms out of the market.

As shown in Table 5, the early years of transition were accompanied by a fall in output which was much deeper and more prolonged than initially predicted, though in most cases this has been followed by recovery. Many of the factors contributing to the initial slump were temporary or one-off, but policies to ensure rapid growth (which is the key to the catching-up process) should remain a major priority in the transition economies.

Explanations for the initial fall in production include the monopoly behaviour of public enterprises (which restricted output and raised prices) and the slow growth of the emerging private sector and/or the failure of official statistics to reflect the growth of that sector adequately. Bruno (1992) also argues that reduced output was the result of a "comprehensive management shock" with the policy disorientation of public enterprises after the collapse of central-planning, and the tendency to adopt a "wait and see" attitude.[12] Output statistics in the former centrally-planned system were exaggerated, and part of the subsequent registered fall in output also reflected a cut in wasteful (if not negative value added) production. Under the previous system, which was characterised by shortage, both enterprises and households held excessive levels of inventories. It was therefore to be expected that there would be a substantial cut in orders for new inputs on the part of firms, and precautionary purchases by households in the early stages of transition (Winiecki, 1995).

The initial fall in output was also the result of external factors such as the collapse of the CMEA trading system[13] (which implied both a supply-side shock with the increase in energy prices, and a fall in the demand for exports from other CMEA countries) and the break-up of the USSR. The war in Yugoslavia and subsequent embargo also led to disruption of trade, in particular in neighbouring Balkan States. The deep recession in West European countries during the early years of transition reduced the demand for exports from the transition economies, while the split of Czechoslovakia led (at least initially) to a dramatic fall in trade between the two new countries.[14]

Table 5 sets out data on unemployment in the CEECs. A low unemployment rate might reflect the ability to create new jobs, or it could simply indicate a lack of progress in transition and the fact that much labour remains to be shed.

Tables 3-5 present some of the main indicators reflecting the macroeconomic performance of the CEECs, and Table 6 represents an attempt to draw these together.

PROGRESS IN MICROECONOMIC RESTRUCTURING
AND PRIVATISATION

Though the questions of macroeconomic performance and progress in transition are intrinsically interlinked, it is useful to shift the emphasis to the questions of microeconomic restructuring, privatisation and institutional change. Microeconomic restructuring entails the correction of the distortions arising from the central control of pricing and the allocation of resources. This is achieved by privatisation, demonopolisation, the end of mandatory planning and the liberalisation of prices, trade and of capital and labour markets.[15] The priorities of the previous system have to be reversed with less emphasis on heavy industry, and a greater role for services (see Table 7 in the appendix) and forms of production which are less intensive in pollution and energy. In order to implement such measures an adequate legal framework with regard to property rights, contracts, competition and company law is also necessary.

As was expected, privatisation was a lengthy and difficult process, but many of the complications which arose had not been foreseen.[16] For instance, in countries such as the Czech Republic which had introduced mass privatisation schemes, investment privitisation funds bought large numbers of shares. In many cases former managers and members of the nomenklatura were also able to gain control of enterprises. These were often less concerned with profit maximization than with "entrenchment" aimed at ensuring the survival of their firm, and own position, if necessary by lobbying politicians and bureaucrats. As a result, the corporate governance of enterprises is emerging as a growing difficulty.

Institutional changes in the financial sphere include the creation of independent central banks, a commercial banking system, and financial markets for bonds and shares. Slow progess in reforming the financial sector is creating difficulties for the operation of monetary instruments in the CEECs. In many cases standard open market operations are impossible, and in some countries there is little competition among banks. There have been various instances of fraud, negligence and financial scandals. Problems also arose from the widespread diffusion of "bad debts" of state enterprises which managed to obtain credit from the state and from each other (in the form of arrears) in order to continue operating and avoid, or at least postpone, bankruptcy. In many cases these state enterprises were backed by government guarantees and were not very sensitive to the price of credit. As Zecchini (1995, p.131) describes, tightening of monetary policy did not prevent the banks supporting these enterprises, or the rapid growth of inter-enterprise credit. Substantial increases in the price of credit often failed to limit credit expansion and frequently meant that small private firms were crowded out as an increasing share of credit went to the large state enterprises.

In assessing progress in microeconomic transformation, a detailed analysis of the economy in question is necessary. Table 8 produced by the European Bank for Reconstruction and Development (EBRD) attempts to bring together and summarise the main indicators of progress in transition. Further indicators could be added to this list such as the rates of growth and of investment, and the ability to reduce unemployment (see Table 5).

Capacity to cope with competitive pressures and market forces within the Community

With regard to capacity to cope with competitive pressures and market forces within the Community, the risk is that with removal of the barriers many firms in the CEECs whose output was destined for the domestic or former CMEA markets would be unable to survive in an enlarged EU market. Against this it can be argued that the CEECs have an advantage as a result of lower wages, but in many cases this is offset by the structural shortcomings of industries.[17]

Although productivity has been increasing in most of the CEECs in recent years, there has been considerable pressure for wage increases, fuelled by the need to raise low living standards. In some cases (and notably the Czech Republic before May 1997), nominal currency stability has undermined the cushion which undervalued exchange rates provided in the early years of transition. One of the results of legislative approximation with EU measures in the areas of social and environmental policies[18] could be to raise production costs in the CEECs.

The question of whether the CEECs will be able to cope with competitive pressures within the Community is rendered particularly acute as it has a sectoral dimension. Sensitive sectors, such as agriculture, textiles, clothing, coal, footwear, steel and chemicals[19] continue to occupy an important position in the CEEC economies. These are the sectors which tend to be characterised by overproduction at a world level, and the present EU members are committed to concerted efforts at reduction of capacity in some of these sectors such as steel and agriculture.[20] Relatively low wages may render the CEECs competitive in the sensitive sectors, but frequently this advantage is offset by structural weaknesses.[21]

Though the Copenhagen criteria refer to the ability of the CEECs to withstand competitive pressures in an enlarged EU, the question also arises for the existing EU(15) member states. The sensitive sectors play an important role in the weaker regions and member states such as Greece and Portugal. With the removal of barriers there is a risk that some of the weaker EU firms would no longer be able to compete with low-cost production in the CEECs, so the EU would experience higher rates of unemployment and closures.[22]

Various arrangements have emerged to meet this fear. For instance, outward processing trade has been used widely in the clothing and textiles industries and this largely accounts for the rapid increase in the CEEC share of extra-EU imports of these products.[23] The share of CEEC exports in extra-EU imports of motor vehicles also rose,[24] partly as a result of the role played by Western subcontracting and investments.

It is difficult not to conclude that, at least in the early years of transition, manufacturing in the CEECs was characterised by inertia, with little strategic adjustment away from the sensitive sectors.[25] Firms tended to act in a defensive way cutting costs and reducing production levels, and investment to alter the pattern of production has been limited (Bofinger, 1995). The CEECs are faced with the urgent task of developing high technology sectors, such as telecommunications. However, as Palankai describes (1996, p. 247), newly established domestic private firms are in a weak position as they have to cope with the "infant industry syndrome" which involves building new capacities, looking for new markets, consolidating management techniques and so on. Foreign direct investment, strategic alliances with Western firms and joint ventures can play a key role in this process.

The importance of such measures finds confirmation in the more recent theories of international trade, advocated *inter alia* by Krugman and Venables (1990). These authors criticise traditional theories of international trade for defining the comparative advantage of a region in terms of natural endowment, and argue that deliberate strategies such as investment in infrastructure, people, and R&D may be more important. National and EU policies may therefore play a key role in determining the shape of an enlarged market.

As will be discussed below, it seems likely that the creation of a larger, less fragmented market will create greater opportunities for investment and growth. A vast literature[26] emerged in connection with the 1992 Single Market Programme illustrating how integration can stimulate competition and technical progress, and enable static and dynamic[27] economies of scale to be exploited. Insofar as enlargement succeeds in creating a more dynamic economic environment, some of the adjustment costs might be eased.

The extent to which integration may contribute to creating a more competitive and dynamic environment will also depend on how far the production of goods appearing in trade is characterised by imperfect competition. The usual indicator taken to assess the share of imperfect competition is the share of intra-industry trade. Intra-industry trade is trade within a single sector, and is generally assumed to be explained by economies of scale and differentiated products. As shown in Table 9 of the appendix, the share of intra-industry trade in EU trade with Slovenia (68% in 1995) and the Visegrad countries is relatively high, but the percentage is much lower for trade with the Baltic States.

In general it is assumed that a higher level of intra-industry imports implies less threat to domestic production because if adjustment is necessary it will be carried out at the level of firms within an industry, or even of production lines within a firm. However, more empirical analysis is necessary to see how far this is the case in practice.[28]

In deciding which economic sectors in which CEECs are ready to cope with competitive pressures and market forces in an enlarged Community, a detailed analysis of their economies is therefore necessary. This could take into account progress in the following areas:

- the creation of a stable and competitive economic environment, *inter alia* through the privatisation process and the introduction of an adequate legal framework with regard to property rights, contracts, competition and company law;

- the evolution of the banking and financial sectors;

- the development of a modern efficient administrative system and a role of the state appropriate to a mixed economy;[29]

- restructuring and modernisation of industries in decline such as coal, steel, agriculture and shipbuilding;

- success in developing industries characterised by growing demand and high technology which are at the core of an information society;

- widening of the industrial base and the diffusion of small and medium enterprises;

— demonopolisation and/or the development of a suitable regulatory framework for sectors dominated by former state-owned enterprises, such as energy and telecommunications;

— the introduction of measures to encourage R&D and technological innovation; and

— measures to promote foreign investment.

Governments in the CEECs are under considerable pressure from producer interests to introduce protectionist measures, and other forms of assistance to enterprises,[30] so care should be taken to resist lobbying activities. As Zielinska-Glebocka (1996) argues, this is a further reason for the importance of coordinating industrial policy with competition policy and trade measures. Trade liberalisation is required by the obligations of the Europe Agreements and Uruguay Round, but the CEECs have a certain amount of leeway in interpreting these obligations.[31] On numerous occasions the CEECs have used the various protective clauses allowed for in the Europe Agreements,[32] even though protectionism is unlikely to prove an efficient instrument in promoting increases in competitiveness.

Adherence to the aim of Economic and Monetary Union

As Daviddi and Ilzkovitz (1996) describe, it is unlikely that the objectives and rules of EMU will be modified for the new CEEC members. Given the time lag before enlargement, if EMU proceeds according to the timetable set out in the Maastricht Treaty, it seems likely that it will be in Stage 3 when the CEECs at the head of the accession list join. As non-participating countries (i.e. with derogations from EMU) during Stage 3 those countries would none the less be obliged to follow rules relating to fiscal discipline, liberalisation of capital movements and the coordination of economic policy. Their central banks would participate in the European System of Central Banks (ESCB), and they would be obliged to ensure the independence of their central banks, and accept the primary objective of price stability. Non-participating countries would, however, be allowed to conduct their own monetary policy and would not be subject to the guidelines of the European Central Bank

(ECB). Member states with derogations would have to participate in some form of exchange rate arrangement with participating countries,[33] but they would not have to completely fix their exchange rate to the euro.

In taking on the *acquis communautaire* with regard to EMU, even as non-participating countries the CEECs would therefore have to accept obligations with regard to price stability, exchange rate stability and fiscal discipline. Given the inflationary pressures associated with transition, the need to cope with capital movements, and the burden imposed by transformation on the budget, these obligations could prove difficult to meet. The loss of the exchange rate instrument and of control of monetary policy implied by full participation in EMU could be even more costly for the CEECs.

The lessons learnt in implementing the IMF-agreed macroeconomic stabilisation programmes in the CEECs could prove useful in this context.[34] Although the IMF generally expressed a preference for fixed nominal exchange rates, the regime actually chosen varied according to the country in question. After substantial devaluations, Poland and Czechoslovakia initially adopted a peg as nominal anchor, while Romania and Bulgaria decided to float as they lacked foreign exchange reserves.[35]

The Czech case proves a good example of the difficulty of attempting to peg the nominal exchange rate in a transition economy.[36] Initially (as was also the case in Poland) the magnitude of the devaluation prevented the exchange rate from acting as an effective anchor. Subsequently, nominal currency stability and a higher rate of inflation than in OECD countries undermined the cushion which an undervalued exchange rate provided in the early years of transition. The real appreciation of the exchange rate was not matched by increases in productivity, and Czech firms began to lose competitiveness. In May 1997 the Czech Republic had to switch to a managed float, based on a target rate of 17-19.5 koruna per D-Mark.

In 1994 and 1995 the combination of a fixed exchange rate and the high interest rates implied by tight monetary policy also led to massive capital inflows into the Czech Republic. Poland and Hungary also experienced capital inflows increasing the demand for domestic currency and rendering money supply targets harder to realise. As a result, for a time all three countries experienced pressure for currency appreciation despite rising current account deficits.[37]

As Gabrisch (1997, pp. 577-580) explains, there are two reasons why the CEECs could experience additional problems in trying to maintain fixed nominal exchange rates after accession. Firstly, the difficulties experienced by certain CEECs as a result of capital inflows could be repeated after enlargement as a consequence of transfers to these countries from the CAP and Structural Funds. Secondly, on the basis of OECD calculations, there are considerable price disparities between the EU and the CEECs.[38] As might be expected, the greatest differences are generally in non-tradables, but among tradables, sectors such as agriculture and clothing with relatively high levels of protection are also the sectors with the largest price disparities.[39] With ongoing trade integration, and the introduction of fixed nominal exchange rates in the CEECs after enlargement, price adjustment to the higher EU levels could be reflected in real appreciation of CEEC currencies.

Acceptance of the 'acquis communautaire' concerning the Single Market

With the opening of accession negotiations with the five front runners in March 1998, the Commission began the process of screening the CEECs to assess their progress in taking on the *acquis communautaire*. It soon became obvious that the complexity of the task had initially been underestimated. The acquis has been expanding steadily and by 1998 comprised some 12,000 legislative acts.

The 1995 White Paper, "Preparation of the Associated Countries of Central and Eastern Europe for Integration into the Internal Market of the Union" had already indicated many of the main tasks to be faced for integration of the CEECs into the Single Market.[40] These entail the elimination of physical, technical, fiscal and tariff barriers between participating states.[41] For that purpose the CEECs will have to put into place and ensure the effective operation "legislation and regulatory systems, standards and certification methods compatible with those of the European Union".[42]

Though the list is not meant to be exhaustive, the regulatory alignment of the CEECs to the internal market requires measures with regard to: health, safety and consumer protection; environmental protection; services, including transport, energy, telecommunications and financial services; customs and indirect taxation; competition policy and social policy.

The White Paper also indicates a sequence for the approximation of legislation. EU support for this process was to be provided through the PHARE Programme and through a new technical assistance information exchange office. The timing and priorities in the introduction of measures are left to the CEECs.

With regard to social policy the aim is to ensure the operation of a "level playing field" and avoid the risk of social dumping. However, Smith et al. (1996, pp. 5-6) argue that social and environmental policy areas should probably not be harmonised prior to accession. To do so is to require the CEECs to accept tighter obligations than existing member states, as in 1989 the UK opted out of the Social Charter and many derogations have been granted for expensive environmental regulations.

An opinion frequently voiced in present EU member states is that a long transition period will be necessary before freedom of movement of labour can be allowed in an enlarged Union. This issue will be taken up in the discussion in Chapter 3 on labour migration, but it is important to point out at this stage that there is an inconsistency between expecting the CEECs to adopt the *acquis* on the Single Market prior to accession, and permitting the EU(15) to delay implementation of one of the fundamental tenets of the internal market (the "four freedoms") after enlargement.

Ability of the CEECs to take on the *acquis* will also be measured according to whether the applicant country has met its obligations under the Europe Agreement. The Europe Agreements committed the CEECs to adopting competition policies compatible with those of the Community and this objective was further specified in the 1995 White Paper.[43] In this context external pressure to force measures which are unpopular, but essential to the transformation process, may play an important role. The introduction of effective anti-trust measures is urgently required in the CEECs, where the legacy of central planning has left a concentrated structure of production, and often privatisation of state enterprises has not been accompanied by adequate measures of demonopolisation. The need to bring legislation in line with that in EU countries in areas such as the control of state aids can provide CEEC governments with a strong justification for resisting excessive rent-seeking on the part of producers.

However, taking on the *acquis communautaire* wholesale is not always appropriate to the conditions of transitional economies. For instance, the EU rules on restrictions on vertical restraints may prove excessively binding in countries attempting to set up adequate distribution networks. Similarly, the exigencies of privatisation and restructuring may require a flexible approach to controls on state aids (Smith et al., 1996).

A full assessment of the degree of regulatory alignment of the CEECs would require a detailed analysis of the state of legislation in each of the CEECs and is beyond the present scope. However, transposition of Single Market measures into national legislation is incomplete even for the existing EU members and, even where national measures have been introduced in the EU (15), these are often inadequate to ensure the objectives of the Single Market.[44]

The political criteria for enlargement[45]

Article 237 of the EEC Treaty and Article O of the Maastricht Treaty specify that "any European state may apply to become a member". Already twenty years ago, there were clearly other conditions: in April 1978, the European Council declared that "respect for and maintenance of representative democracy and human rights in each Member State are essential elements of membership in the European Communities."[46] In a report on enlargement to the June 1992 Lisbon European Council, the Commission argued that there are "three basic conditions of European identity, democratic status, and respect of human rights."[47]

With regards to the most recent enlargement, there was no doubt that Austria, Finland, and Sweden were democratic and respected human rights. Three countries, Greece, Spain, and Portugal, had previously joined the Community following a transition to democracy. Specific membership requirements for them were not spelt out, but certainly included genuine free elections, the right balance of party strength (pro-democracy parties in the ascendence), and a reasonably stable government. A long negotiation period allowed the Community time to ensure that democracy was being consolidated in the three states.[48]

The CEECs have also applied for Union membership during a process of democratisation and political reform. From the late 1980s, the Community/Union has made trade concessions, aid, and association agreements for the CEECs conditional on progress in economic and political reforms, as a means of encouraging the transition. Following this, the Copenhagen European Council in June 1993 accepted that the Central and East European associates could join the Union, but indicated several conditions that prospective members must meet.

There are essentially three "political" conditions. The applicants must have achieved stability of institutions guaranteeing democracy, the rule of law, human rights and respect for and protection of minorities. They must be able to take on the obligations of membership, including adherence to the aims of political union. In addition, the Union would have to be able to absorb new members and maintain the momentum of integration.

The conditions are a very important means of influencing the Central and East European associates: the EU thus exerts pressure on the associates to carry out reforms and behave as good neighbours.[49] In this context, providing a date for enlargement would be counterproductive, because enlargement could take place only once the conditions have been fulfilled. But there are problems with applying conditionality, as discussed below. It may not be compatible with political stability, which is, after all, one of the EU's objectives in Eastern Europe.

It should be noted that the CEECs have received less EU financial assistance to help them meet the political criteria than they have to help them carry out the necessary economic reforms. PHARE, through the Democracy Programme and other programmes, has helped to build institutions and civil society in the CEECs. But the amount of aid for such programmes is small: the PHARE Democracy Programme totals ECU 10 million, but PHARE's yearly budget tops ECU 1 billion.[50] This is now changing: in March 1997, the Commission approved new PHARE orientations to channel more funds (30% of total PHARE resources) for strengthening democratic institutions and public administrations in the applicant countries.

There is a considerable degree of "subjectivity" in the EU's conditions. The aims of political union are hard to accept if "political union" remains undefined; certainly the current member states would not agree on its meaning. Whether the EU can absorb new members and maintain the momentum of integration is also a matter of interpretation. Within the EU, there does not seem to be a clear idea about the future shape and orientation of a larger Union. More "flexibility" is widely considered necessary, but the exact form that flexibility will take remains undefined, despite the Amsterdam European Council conclusions (see section 1 of Chapter 3). Judging the fulfilment of these conditions is thus difficult. Several member states (and the Commission) have insisted that the EU must be reformed fundamentally before enlargement can occur.

Acceptance of the so-called *acquis politique* is included in the membership obligations, but exactly what it consists of is a bit vague. It certainly includes the Maastricht Treaty (with Common Foreign and Security Policy provisions) and its political objectives,[51] but may be limited to acceptance of the procedures of foreign policy cooperation, not the statements and policies already agreed.[52] This should not be problematic for the CEECs, and accepting past statements and policies could reassure outsiders (particularly those with whom the CEECs have had difficult relations) that the EU's current approach towards a given country will continue along more or less the same lines.

The condition of stable democratic institutions guaranteeing the rule of law and respect for human and minority rights is perhaps less subject to manipulation.[53] Several "yardsticks" are available for judging whether the applicant countries meet this condition. The European Bank for Reconstruction and Development also applies political conditionality and has compiled a list of factors that are relevant for judging the state of democracy in recipient countries (see Table 12). Human rights indicators could be found in the European Convention on Human Rights and, particularly, the Council of Europe Framework Convention for the Protection of National Minorities (see Table 13). Obviously, progress on meeting the democracy condition involves not just changing formal constitutions and laws, but following democratic principles and respecting human rights in practice.[54]

In its July 1997 opinions on the membership applications, the Commission looked at a variety of detailed criteria: the democratic principles embodied in constitutions, the workings of democratic institutions (including elections), freedom of expression and association, and respect for minorities.[55] While the extent to which each applicant meets the political conditions is beyond the scope of the present paper, possible problems can be indicated.

Kaldor and Vejvoda (1997) have found that, for the most part, all ten applicant countries meet formal criteria of democracy (including rule of law, free elections, separation of powers, and freedom of expression). But in all ten countries, progress is slower in meeting substantive criteria, including the character of constitutions, the role of political parties, the role of the media, and the existence of an active civil society. The Commission also noted that all the applicant states have flaws in the rule of law, lack qualified judges and do not have sufficient guarantees of judicial independence, and need to improve the training and discipline of their police forces, while several states should provide a firmer legal basis for local government autonomy.[56]

Three countries in particular have appeared to be behind in their fulfilment of the democracy condition: Slovakia, Bulgaria, and Romania. Bulgaria and Romania have recently undergone a period of political instability, but after the most recent elections, seem to be more on track towards democratic stability. Slovakia, however, remains a concern. The EU has had occasion over the past three years to remind Slovakia that it will not join the EU unless it proceeds with democratisation and protects human and minority rights.[57] The Commission in fact recommended excluding Slovakia from membership negotiations because it does not fulfill the democracy condition and does not adequately protect minority rights.

The protection of minority rights should be one of the most important factors taken into account in assessing the membership applications. A likely source of instability within the associates is inter-ethnic tension. Disputes and conflicts are possible between them as a result of one state's concern over the treatment of ethnic minorities in a neighbouring state. Disputes over territory could arise in part from minority grievances - states might want to change their boundaries to include more of their dominant ethnic group within their state.[58]

Insisting on the protection of minority rights, though, is problematic. States fear that by granting substantial autonomy to minorities, they create a precedent for separation. By granting rights on the basis of ethnic or other exclusionary criteria, states perpetuate divisions. Minority rights and individual human rights may not be compatible. EU member states themselves are divided over the concept of minority rights, with France and the UK more inclined to emphasise individual rights.

Inter-ethnic relations have been difficult within several of the applicant countries, and have been a source of problems in their relations with each other. Relations between Hungary, Slovakia and Romania have been seriously strained over the treatment of Hungarian minorities, among other issues.[59] In March 1996 the Slovak parliament passed a law on state language which did not include the possibility that minorities could use their own language in areas where they constitute a substantial part of the population.[60] In Romania, anti-Hungarian, anti-Semitic and racist parties were close to or part of the government in

1994-1996. In the summer of 1995, the Romanian government blamed ethnic Hungarians for atrocities committed during the 1989 revolution and limited minority language rights. Following several warnings from Western States, President Jon Iliescu launched an initiative for reconciliation with Hungary. The new government, in power since November 1996, includes a minister from the Hungarian Democratic Union party. In Estonia and Latvia, the treatment of Russians living in those countries (with particular respect to the different provisions on citizenship) has attracted Western attention. The Commission's opinions on the membership applications express considerable concern about the treatment of the Hungarian minority in Slovakia, and much less about the treatment of non-citizens (generally Russians) in Estonia and Latvia.

To try to reduce disputes over minorities, the EU has strongly encouraged the East European countries to cooperate with each other, but this is not officially a membership condition.[61] The Pact on Stability in Europe has been by far the EU's most important initiative to foster regional cooperation and the protection of minority rights. This was a series of conferences and roundtables between May 1994 and March 1995, in which the associates (minus Slovenia, which had not yet signed an association agreement with the EU) were urged to conclude good neighbour agreements covering the problems of national minorities and borders, and to set up regional cooperation arrangements. Although the EU did not explicitly state that participation was a membership condition, many of the associates agreed (reluctantly) to the Pact because they considered it a condition. Hungary and Slovakia reached a good-neighbourly agreement within the framework of the Pact in March 1995, but Slovakia did not ratify it until a year later and relations between the two countries remain tense (particularly over the issue of Slovakia's treatment of its Hungarian minority). Hungary and Romania signed a treaty in September 1996 though relations are still difficult. The Pact still does not contain good-neighbourly agreements between Russia and Estonia or Latvia.

Border disputes between the applicant countries, and with other outside countries, are also a matter of concern. The Commission (1997, p. 45) maintains that all applicant countries should make every effort to resolve outstanding border disputes before they accede to the Union. All the countries should commit themselves to submit all border disputes to the International Court of Justice.

But the issue of regional cooperation among the associates remains a concern: even the three countries considered most likely to join the EU in the first wave, the Czech Republic, Hungary, and Poland, do not readily or easily cooperate with each other. The three countries and Slovakia did set up the Central European Free-Trade Agreement (CEFTA) in 1992.[62] There are several other regional groupings in Central and Eastern Europe that link the associates with EU member states and other non-applicant countries, but the overriding concern of the applicant states remains that of joining the EU.[63] Some associates have claimed that the EU's encouragement of regional cooperation is an attempt to block their accession to the EU because a separate regional grouping could serve as an alternative to EU membership.[64] But EU membership requires that member states cooperate with each other (obviously). The CEECs "will be rather surprised to find that the parallel integration of neighbouring countries with the European centre automatically means close links with each other too."[65]

Given the implications of enlargement in stages for relations between the newly enlarged EU and outsiders, the state of relations between the applicant countries, and between the applicant countries and other countries in the region, should be an important consideration in making enlargement decisions. The better the relations among the CEECs before enlargement, the less likely it is that enlargement will be seen as a divisive and exclusive process.

Notes

1 Agenda 2000, p. 42.
2 How seriously these criteria are being taken is evident, for example, from the case of Poland where the new constitution introduced rules fixing the maximum levels of public deficit and debt at the Maastricht levels.
3 As the Christodoulou Report (1996) of the European Parliament (Annex I, p. 17) points out, this is particularly likely to be the case if CEECs have not completed structural reforms, introduced sound economic and fiscal policies and achieved a satisfactory level of convergence.
4 Andreff (1997) notes the distinction between nominal (as measured by the Maastricht criteria) and real convergence. Real convergence refers to the ability to "close the gap", or to reduce long-term disparities in standards of living. The indicators of real convergence include GDP growth, and trends in unemployment, productivity and investment. Real convergence may also be taken to refer to socio-economic variables such as education, health care and life expectancy, as well as the microeconomic variables indicating structural and institutional change.

According to Andreff, 1997, (p.1) "the price to pay for nominal convergence might well be a stagnation widening the gap with other countries (divergence) as far as real macroeconomic variables are concerned". He cites Fayolle (1996) who describes how Spain experienced rapid catching up over the 1986-92 period, but after 1992/3 when nominal criteria began to prevail in macroeconomic policy, real expansion began to slow down. Andreff (1997, p.7) also points to the fact that the Czech Republic, which appears to perform best among the CEECs in terms of nominal convergence, lags behind other countries such as Hungary and Estonia (and possibly also Poland) in terms of economic restructuring.

5   See also Figure 1.
6   Council for Mutual Economic Assistance or Comecon. See Senior Nello 1991 for a description of the activities of this organisation.
7   The discount rate is defined as the rate at which monetary institutes lend or discount eligible paper for deposit money banks. The lending rate is used to meet the short-run and medium-run financing needs of the private sector.
8   In April 1991 the Paris Club agreed to debt relief on some 50% of Polish debt which was backed by Western governments, reducing the total from $33.7 billion to $18 billion over five years.
9   UN/ECE, *Economic Bulletin for Europe*, vol. 47 (1995).
10 A further difficulty could arise from the high share of budgetary redistribution in GDP. According to Palankai (1996) this amounted to 60% for Hungary in 1993, compared with 40-45% in Western Europe, and 46% for the Czech Republic.
11 If governments take advantage of the temporary trade off between inflation and unemployment and raise inflation to reduce unemployment, agents will come to expect them to do so and will predict a higher level of inflation. What is needed is a way of making commitment to lower inflation credible, and an independent European Central Bank commited to curbing inflation may perform this function and bring about a lower rate of inflation. In this way the inflation-prone country may "borrow" credibility.
12 After 1989 enterprise managers who were used to operating in a command economy, where their market was assured, and financing was accommodative, had to adapt to a transformed, and very uncertain environment.
13 Rodrik (1993) has estimated total losses in output due to collapse in the CMEA in the order of 30-50% in 1991-1992.
14 According to Drábek (1995), in 1993 the real value of Czech exports to Slovakia fell by 23% in 1993.
15 For a more detailed discussion of these questions see Senior Nello (1991 and forthcoming).
16 For a recent survey of privatisation in the CEECs see Uvalic, M. and Vaughan-Whitehead, D. (1997).
17 For instance, as the EC Commission's Agricultural Strategy Paper (1995), p. 7, argues, despite lower labour costs, inefficiencies in food processing and distribution mean that a doubling or more of wheat prices between the farm gate and the border is not exceptional in many of the CEECs.
18 This issue will be taken up in the next section.
19 The inclusion of chemicals among the sensitive sectors is justified by the large share of EU anti-dumping measures in this sector, but it is not accepted by all authors. For instance in CEPR (1992) chemicals are not included in the list of sensitive sectors.
20 For example the CAP has involved production quotas for sugar since 1968, and for

milk since 1984. In addition, set-aside, or the policy of leaving land uncultivated was first introduced in 1988, and its use was greatly extended by the MacSharry reform of 1992.

21 For instance, as the EC Commission's Agricultural Strategy Paper (1995, p.7) argues, despite lower labour costs, inefficiencies in food processing and distribution mean that a doubling or more of wheat prices between the farm gate and the border is not exceptional in many of the CEECs.

22 Cadot and de Melo (1995) have used estimates of a gravity model, and extrapolations of observed structural developments to analyse whether increased imports from the CEECs are likely to result in job destruction in the EU. Their simulations suggest an upper limit of some 13,000 jobs being lost in the EU, with very little regional concentration (apart from some 850 jobs being lost in coal production in Lorraine).

23 CEEC(6) share of extra-EU imports of these products rose from 7% for each group in 1989, to 13% and 14% respectively in 1994 (UN/ECE, *Economic Survey of Europe 1995-1996*).

24 The share of CEEC(6) exports in extra-EU imports of motor vehicles increased to 5.3% in 1994 (UN/ECE, *Economic Survey of Europe 1995-1996*).

25 As Drábek and Smith (1995) illustrate for Poland, the Czech Republic, and Hungary, if agriculture is excluded from the analysis, the share of remaining sensitive products in total exports has been rising.

26 Including Emerson et al (1989) and the Cecchini Report.

27 Learning effects reflecting the role of experience. As cumulative output increases over time, the unit costs of a firm decline.

28 The distinction between vertical intra-industry trade (involving quality differences) and horizontal intra-industry trade (which is trade in genuinely similar products) might prove useful in this context.

29 This involves a reduction in state ownership and the use of direct controls, but it should not be taken to imply that transition can simply be achieved by the withdrawal of the state. This misconception led to the problem of "desertification" in many of the CEECs in the early 1990s.

30 The Hungarian economist, Kornai (1980, 1986) has described the network which linked "the paternalistic state and the firm which is its client" in the central-planning system, and it appears that transition has not been completely successful in breaking down this type of "tutelage" relationship.

31 As discussed in the section on trade in Chapter 3.

32 For instance, Poland used general safeguards for balance of payments purposes in 1993 and 1996, and for motor vehicles in 1994. In 1994 tariffs were imposed on telecommunications on the basis of the infant industry argument, and in 1996 protective measures were imposed on petrochemical imports on the basis of the restructuring clause (Zielinska-Glebocka, 1996).

33 The most likely institutional framework would be a new European Monetary System (EMS II). Whatever form this takes, countries not fully participating in EMU are unlikely to be allowed to devalue their exchange rates unilaterally.

34 The model for IMF-agreed stabilisation programmes in the transition economies was the Polish Balcerowicz Plan which came into effect from 1 January 1990. Subsequently other transition countries (including Czechoslovakia, Bulgaria and Romania at the beginning of 1991) introduced similar stabilisation programmes. The main elements of these programmes were:
– rapid and almost complete price liberalisation;

- restrictive monetary and credit policies;
- tight fiscal discipline, and the wide scale elimination of price subsidies;
- substantial trade liberalisation;
- incomes policies. In Poland, Hungary and Romania, tax-based incomes policies were introduced, while in Bulgaria real wages were cut by 35% and ceilings on wage bills were introduced.
- privatisation; and
- the reform of the banking and financial systems.

35 In 1997 Romania and Bulgaria were still floating (though on a number of occasions their central banks had intervened on foreign exchange markets), while Poland, Hungary, Slovenia and (from May) the Czech Republic opted for managed floating. Estonia and Lithuania had currency boards.
36 Initially the koruna's exchange rate was based on a basket made up of the dollar and D-mark.
37 See Gabrisch (1997) for a description of these effects.
38 Macroeconomic price disparities are generally calculated with the help of purchasing power parities (PPPs). PPPs measure the cost of a comparable basket of goods and services in national currencies using the exchange rate. The comparative price level index is given by the reciprocal of the so-called exchange rate deviation index, i.e. the ratio of the exchange rate to PPP. According to Gabrisch (1995, pp. 579-580), with Germany as 100, the comparative price level indices at 1993 GDP were as follows: Hungary 50, Poland 38, Slovakia and the Czech Republic 28, Bulgaria and Romania 25, Estonia 23, Latvia 22 and Lithuania 16.
39 Taking Austria as 100, according to Gabrisch (1995, p.580) the overall comparative price index for Poland in 1993 was 39.9, but, for example, the index was 44.3 for food, 47.1 for clothing, 19.2 for rent and energy, 49.7 for furniture and household effects, 22.8 for medical treatment, 55.5 for transport and telecommunications, 27.7 for recreation and education and 51.5 for other goods and services.
40 The Single Market is defined as an area without internal frontiers in which the four freedoms (of movement of goods, services, people and capital) are ensured.
41 One way of eliminating the barriers to movement of goods and services would be to introduce common rules and regulations. However, the detailed, technical legislation that this involves is likely to prove too complex and costly, as well as running the risks of excessive uniformity and bureaucratic interference. To meet this difficulty the Community relies so far as possible on the principle of mutual recognition (established in the famous *Cassis de Dijon* case of 1979), according to which all goods lawfully manufactured and marketed in one member country should be accepted also in other member countries. Exceptions related to public health, the fairness of commercial transactions and the defence of the consumer are permitted. The introduction of the Single Market also has to respect the principle of subsidiarity whereby legislation at the Community level should only be introduced where the same or a better effect cannot be achieved at a regional or national level.
42 Conclusions of the European Council at Essen, 9 and 10 December 1994, SN 300/94, p. 13.
43 The White Paper makes reference to Articles 85, 86 and 90 relating to competition rules, and Article 92 concerning state aids.
44 Progress in implementing the Single Market in the EU (15) appears to be particularly slow with regard to public procurement, the recognition of higher education diplomas, and (at least in certain EU states) the liberalisation of air transport, energy, telecommunications, and financial services.

45 The following section draws in part on K. Smith (1998 forthcoming), chapters 6 and 7.
46 "Declaration on Democracy", Copenhagen European Council, 7-8 April 1978, *EC Bulletin* no. 3, 1978, p. 6.
47 This is because two essential characteristics of the EU (as stated in article F of the Maastricht Treaty) are democracy and respect of fundamental human rights. EC Commission (1992), p. 11.
48 Pridham (1994), p. 24. While the Commission discussed (briefly) the transition to democracy in its opinions on the three states, it did so in general terms. But clearly Community membership was linked to the consolidation of democracy in those countries, as stated in the "Opinion on Greek Application for Membership", EC Commission (1976), p. 9. See also EC Commission (1978a) and (1978b).
49 Mathias Jopp has argued that "conditions for accession, together with a realistic perspective for membership, are the most effective lever for the Union to influence developments in Central and Eastern Europe." Jopp (1994), pp. 58-59. See also Munuera (1994), pp. 91-92.
50 Tables 10 and 11 of the appendix provide estimates of financial assistance to the CEECs.
51 Agenda 2000, vol. 1, p. 42.
52 This was the case with Greece's acceptance of the EPC *acquis*. Nuttall (1992), pp. 173-174. But Anna Michalski and Helen Wallace (1992) argue that the *acquis* seems to include adoption of CFSP shared policies (p. 21).
53 All ten associates belong to the Council of Europe, whose statutory principles are pluralist democracy, respect for human rights and the rule of law.
54 And the European Commission (1997, p. 33) stated that it assessed how democracy works in practice in each applicant state.
55 Agenda 2000, vol. 1, pp. 41-45.
56 Agenda 2000, vol. 1, p. 43.
57 In November 1994 and October 1995, the EU presented démarches to the Slovak government, reiterating that Slovakia's relations with the EU depended on its progress in implementing democratic norms. In November 1995, the European Parliament threatened to suspend aid to Slovakia because of violations of human and minority rights, and disregard for the rule of law. In February 1997, Commissioner Hans van den Broek urged Slovakia to approve a law on the use of minority languages.
58 See Walker (1993), p. 45.
59 There are approximately 600,000 ethnic Hungarians in Slovakia and 100,000 ethnic Slovaks in Hungary. Romania has between 1.6 and 2 million ethnic Hungarians. Hungary's attitude on the minorities issue has not always been constructive (particularly under the Antall government 1990-94): it has argued that is has a special obligations towards Hungarians living outside Hungary. See "Minorities: That Other Europe", *The Economist*, 25 December 1993-7 January 1994. In 1992-1993, the Commission mediated another dispute between Slovakia and Hungary, over the Gabcikovo dam project on the Danube. See Munuera 1994, pp. 8-11.
60 See Batt (1996), pp. 29-34.
61 The multilateral political dialogue between the Community/Union and the associates, initiated in 1992 with the Visegrad countries, clearly was devised to spur regional cooperation. The dialogue developed into the structured relationship, which is likewise a multilateral framework. PHARE aid has been channelled into regional cooperation programmes and cross-national projects. But it should be noted that

these efforts contrast with and contradict the bilateral framework for economic and political relations set up by the Europe agreements.
62 Slovenia joined CEFTA in January 1996; other associates (Bulgaria, Lithuania and Romania), as well as Ukraine, are also to join. See "Concrete Heads", *The Economist*, 16 September 1995, and *European Report* no. 2206, 12 March 1997.
63 One such grouping is the Central European Initiative, an Italian initiative originally called the Pentagonale.
64 See Körmendy (1992), p. 248 and Adamcic (1993), pp. 24-25.
65 Balázs (1995), p. 16.

3 Consequences of Enlargement in Stages

Institutional implications

The institutional implications of further enlargement are well known. In general, if decision-making procedures are not reformed, a larger EU could result in slower or blocked decisions. This would particularly be the case where decisions must be taken by unanimity, for example, in Maastricht Treaty pillars two (Common Foreign and Security Policy) and three (Justice and Home Affairs). With enlargement, there could be more "lowest-common-denominator" decision-making, or a failure to act at all. Greater recourse to qualified majority voting seems to be called for, but is controversial among the current member states, and there are reasons to doubt whether the Central and East European states would accept this.

Many of the Central and East European associates are also new states, arising from the break-up of federations in the early 1990s, or in any case, are states whose borders date only from the end of World War I. "In these circumstances, the symbolic abolition or even the transparency of state borders through integration is a rather sensitive and actual question in Eastern Europe."[1] All new member states must adjust to membership in a "supranational" institution, but this may be particularly difficult for countries which have so recently "regained" sovereignty.

In addition to the effects of enlargement on formal decision-making procedures, an increase in the number of member states has other, perhaps even more far-reaching, effects. It will take time to integrate the new member states into "policy networks", which will affect policy-making.[2] Enlargement will inevitably influence any development of "community" feeling and solidarity within the EU. Even where unanimous voting is required, member states have refrained from vetoing measures, because they could be reasonably sure of benefiting from similar actions by other member states in the future. An increase in the EU's membership could alter the decision-making style from the (at least occasional) use of a problem-solving approach, which relies on a sense of common values, to the much more prevalent use of bargaining or confrontation.[3] The "Community method" (which involves the willingness of member states to make compromises) could come under considerable strain. The socialization of new member states will take time, assuming that socialization can occur in a larger, more diverse group (although enlargement in stages does mean that the group will grow larger more gradually). This could negatively affect EU decision-making. Member states that feel bound by a stronger sense of solidarity and community could be tempted to strengthen their links, forming a "hard core".

The EU's institutions should be adapted to cope with a larger Union. The number of Members of European Parliament (MEPs) should be limited if the Parliament is not to expand indefinitely (but this could increase the imbalance in the electoral base of MEPs from large and small member states). The number of Commissioners and European Court of Justice judges would also have to be restricted, possibly to less than the total number of member states. The enlargement of the Council, particularly to more small member states, raises questions about the relative voting weight of the small member states and the threshold of votes needed to approve measures by qualified majority.[4] Tables 14 and 15 and Figure 2 give an indication of the effects that enlargement could have on the current voting arrangements in the Council. The poorer member states would gain considerable voting power (providing they vote together), which could result in wrangles over the budget in particular. Member states would hold the rotating presidency less often, and even the troika (of the past, present and future presidencies) would be perceived as weak if the presidency were held by a succession of small states. With enlargement, the number of official languages will also rise (as will the costs of translating and interpreting), unless other arrangements are made, such as adopting working languages.

There is a danger that none or only some of the institutional and decision-making reforms considered necessary will be undertaken. Because enlargement in stages implies that only a few states will join at a time (and may join different policies with different transition periods), the sense that EU institutions and decision-making procedures must be reformed urgently could be diminished.[5] If this is the case, then the

Union could experience paralysis (to a greater extent than critics claim occurs now).

The 1996-97 IGC was to have agreed on the reforms needed for enlargement to Central and Eastern Europe. But the Amsterdam European Council in June 1997, which concluded the IGC, largely put off tough decisions on reforms. Under the Amsterdam Treaty, qualified majority voting was extended to a few more areas. With the first stage of enlargement, the large member states will give up one of their Commissioners, but only if the weights of the votes in the Council are readjusted. If the first stage of enlargement includes more than five countries, however, this compromise would have to be reconsidered. Furthermore, the Amsterdam European Council concluded that a new revision of the EU's institutions will be necessary to prepare for a second wave of enlargement, which will bring the EU's membership to over twenty member states.

EU enlargement will entail changes in the membership of the Western European Union (WEU), the EU's putative "defense arm" since the Maastricht Treaty.[6] Those states that join both NATO and the EU could become full WEU members,[7] those states that join the EU but not NATO could become observers (which is, broadly speaking, the status of the neutral EU member states). But the forms of WEU membership may need to be changed, since WEU associate membership (for NATO members that are not also EU member states) seems to allow for greater participation in the WEU than does observer status. New member states may thus not be satisfied with observer status. Differing memberships in the EU, WEU and NATO may further complicate - or even block - decision-making in the foreign policy, security, and defense fields. It could also preclude eventual decisions on an EU-WEU merger, as envisaged in the Amsterdam Treaty, because that could give non-NATO members a security guarantee "through the back door".

Implications for budgetary expenditures and receipts

The extent and speed of acceptance of the *acquis communautaire* by new members has always constituted a central difficulty for successive EU enlargements. In the case of eastward enlargement the large number of applicants, their relatively low level of income (the increase in EU population would far exceed the addition to GDP as shown in Table 16), and the fact that most CEECs have large agricultural sectors pose particular difficulties. One of the key questions which arises concerns how far enlargement in stages will ease the problem of extending the structural funds and the Common Agricultural Policy (CAP) to the CEECs.

Additional spending through the Structural Funds

As Table 17 illustrates, with the exception of Slovenia, the per capita GDP in terms of dollars of the CEECs was far below that of the poorest EU (15) member states. When comparing per capita income in the CEECs and EU it is essential to bear in mind the limitations of comparisons of this type. All the CEECs have rapidly growing private sectors, much of which fails to show up in official statistics, though it must be recalled that most EU economies also have substantial "informal" sectors. A second difficulty arises in that the prices of non-traded relative to traded goods tend to be lower in poorer countries. For this reason comparisons of per capita income are often made on the basis of purchasing power parity (PPP). However, as Table 17 shows, even using this measure, per capita income in the CEECs is lower than in the existing EU.

Despite the rapid growth of the CEECs, it appears likely that it will take some years to eliminate the income disparity compared with existing EU member states. Baldwin (1994) estimates that even with 5% growth, the catch up period ranges from 8 years for Slovenia to 22 years for Poland and 26 years for Slovakia.

Table 18 sets out the various estimates of the cost of extending the Structural Funds[8] to the CEECs. According to Courchene et al. (1993), the financial perspective for the 1994-99 period agreed at the Edinburgh summit entailed a commitment of per capita support to the two poorest countries (Greece and Portugal) of 400 ECU per capita in 1999. Given the "relative backwardness and evident lack of modern infrastructure"[9] of the CEECs, a transfer of 400 ECU per capita would seem a minimum claim. However, if applied to the four Visegrad countries, it would imply an increase in structural spending of 26 billion ECU, while, according to Grabbe and Hughes (1998), extension of the structural funds at 400 UCU per capita to the CEEC (10) would imply an additional expenditure of 42 billion ECU per year.

Brenton and Gros (1993) estimate the cost of extending Structural Funds to the CEECs both on the basis of the 1992 rate of aid per capita to the poorest EC country, Greece, and on the basis of the projected

1999 rates per head, allowing for a 43.5% increase in Objective 1 expenditure. The latter estimates are based on the assumption that GDP grows in all countries by 2.5% (i.e. that there is no catching up). Fayolle and Le Cacheux (1995) provide an alternative estimate which also takes into account levels of unemployment in beneficiary states, and their results are also presented in Table 18.[10]

The European Council in Edinburgh set the EU's total budget for economic and social cohesion at 0.46% of EU GDP for the period 1994-99. In Agenda 2000 the Commission proposed maintaining that percentage for the 2000-2006 period. The Commission envisaged spending 275,000 million ECU (at 1997 prices) on the Structural and Cohesion Funds for the years 2000-2006 compared with 200,000 million ECU over the 1994-99 period. A proposed 45,000 million would be earmarked for enlargement. This would consist of 1 billion each year for the CEECs over the 2000-2006 period as part of the pre-accession strategy, and 38 billion from the structural and cohesion funds for the new member states. As a result, by 2006 the Structural Funds for enlargement would account for about 30% of all transfers through the Structural Funds.[11]

However, realisation of the Commission's proposals concerning spending on economic and structural cohesion for the CEECs rests on two fundamental assumptions:

– that the present main recipients of the structural funds in the EU (15) are prepared to accept the reallocation of part of the transfers towards the CEECs;[12] and

– that the relatively optimistic predictions concerning growth rates[13] in the EU(15) and CEECs which underlie the estimates presented in Agenda 2000 are borne out in practice.

Extension of the Structural Funds to the CEECs also requires profound changes in the way in which the Funds operate in practice.[14] Accession of the CEECs would lower the average GDP of the Community so some countries which currently benefit from Objective 1 assistance would no longer qualify. According to Brenton and Gros (1993), in order to enable existing beneficiaries to continue receiving aid, the threshold would have to become 92% of the average GDP per capita in an enlarged Community comprising Bulgaria, Romania, the Visegrad countries and Baltic states.

To meet this difficulty, and to simplify the operation of the structural funds, in Agenda 2000 the Commission proposed reducing the number of Objectives to three. Objective 1 would apply to regions whose GDP is less than 75% of the EU average. Objective 2 concerns regions with major economic and social restructuring needs. Objective 3 would be a "horizontal" measure concerned with the development of human capital, and applying in all regions not covered by Objectives 1 and 2. Its aim would be to help member states adapt and modernise their education, training and employment. Mechanisms to improve monitoring of implementation would also be improved, and Community initiatives would be fewer and more concentrated. There would be increased recourse to financial instruments other than grants (i.e. loans, equity participation etc.).[15]

In Agenda 2000 the Commission refers to a "phasing out mechanism" for regions currently eligible for Objective 1, but which would be above the 75% threshold in an enlarged EU. Again, it remains to be seen how far the poorer regions of the existing EU(15) are prepared to accept sacrifices in the interests of enlargement.

The conditions of partnership and additionality also pose difficulties for extension of the Structural Funds to the CEECs.[16] Partnership entails cooperation between the Commission and national, regional and local authorities in programming structural spending. The principle of subsidiarity entails that where possible regional authorities should be responsible for the implementation of structural measures. However, the centralised political system which characterised the central-planning system means that often the CEECs have little experience of regional devolution of authority.

The principle of additionality is aimed at ensuring that Community funds do not simply replace national expenditure, and requires that Community measures are accompanied by matching funding from the member states of up to 50%. The estimated transfers from extending the structural funds on present criteria to the CEECs would represent an extremely high percentage of the GDP of these countries. According to a study carried out by the Commission (1996b), these transfers would amount to 15% of GDP for Hungary, 18% for the Czech and Slovak Republics, 25% for Poland, and roughly 50% for Romania and Bulgaria. To meet the problems of absorption, Agenda 2000 therefore proposed placing a ceiling of 4% of the GDP of the recipient country on the size of the transfer to CEECs joining the EU.

The results presented here suggest that enlargement in stages reduces the problem of extending structural funds to the CEECs, but does not render it less intractable. Furthermore enlargement in stages also encounters the difficulty posed by the huge discrepancy between transfers under the structural funds (see Table 19 and Figure 3) and the far smaller amount of funds available for the PHARE Programme (see Tables 10 and 11) and proposed in Agenda 2000 for the pre-accession strategy. There is a risk that CEECs joining the EU would be able to benefit from substantial spending from the Structural Funds, while CEECs remaining outside the first wave(s) of enlargement would receive far lower transfers. The Commission's proposal to reinforce the pre-accession strategy with transfers through the Structural Funds would help to reduce (but not remove) this discrepancy. Permitting CEECs excluded from the first round of enlargement to benefit from transfers from the Structural Funds as part of the pre-accession strategy would have the advantage of enabling these countries to gain some experience of working with Community policies before joining the EU.

Additional spending on the CAP

There have been numerous studies of the expected impact of extending the CAP to the CEECs on the EU budget, and the result of some of these are summarised in Table 20. The results are generally presented for the Visegrad 4, and (sometimes) the Balkan 2 and the Baltic 3, rather than being broken down by individual country. The differences between the various estimates are largely to be explained in terms of different predictions concerning the future levels of production and consumption in the CEECs, and the extent to which the effects of the 1992 MacSharry Reform and the Uruguay Round Agreement are taken into account.

According to the estimates presented in Agenda 2000, the costs to the EU budget of extending the CAP to the 10 CEECs would amount to 17.8 billion over the 2000-2006 period. This would consist of 0.5 billion ECU (rising to 0.6 billion ECU from 2002) each year in pre-accession aid, while new member states would receive a total of 6.2 billion ECU for market organisation measures (in particular for the dairy sector) and 7.6 billion ECU for rural development accompanying measures over the 2002-2006 period.[17]

However, the estimates presented in Agenda 2000 are based on the assumption that a radical reform of the CAP will be implemented. This would entail a 20% reduction in the intervention price for cereals, reductions in market support prices of dairy products by 10% (the suggested cut being increased to 15% in the March 1998 proposals of the Commission), and cuts of 30% in the support prices for beef. Farmers in the EU(15) would be compensated for these price cuts through direct payments. Milk quotas would continue until 2006 and compulsory set-aside would be set at zero.

In the past the farm lobby in the Community has proved itself extremely resilient in resisting attempts at CAP reform.[18] Also on this occasion it seems likely that EU farmers will organise vigorous opposition to cuts in guaranteed support prices, even if these are accompanied by compensatory payments. Beef farmers, in particular, are unlikely to be amenable to the sacrifices requested of them, given the difficulties they have experienced in recent years with BSE (the "mad cow" disease). Farmers dislike compensatory payments which appear like charity. Moreover, there is uncertainty concerning how long the compensatory payments will continue, and the use of direct aid has the added inconvenience of rendering the scale of transfers to farmers more transparent. Farmers in the CEECs are also unlikely to appreciate the discrepancy in treatment with regard to direct income payments in an enlarged EU.

The estimates for CAP spending presented in Agenda 2000 therefore have to be interpreted as an opening move by the Commission in what is likely to prove a protracted bargaining process. The final outcome will be a compromise and it is doubtful that the costs of extending the CAP to the CEECs will mirror closely the financial perspective for the years 2000-2006 set out in Agenda 2000.

Returning to the problem of the relative burden to CAP spending of the different CEECs, Table 21 indicates the land area, agricultural population, level of production, and the extent to which agricultural output is absorbed by the country or exported in each of the CEEC (10). Table 22 shows the percentage increase which would result if 1994 levels of production of some of the principal agricultural products in the CEECs are added to the 1994 level of output of those products in the EU(15) in order to provide a very rough indication[19] of how the addition burden of CAP spending might vary according to the CEEC in question.

What emerges from the discussion here is that enlargement in waves fails to resolve the problem of extending the CAP to the CEECs. Three countries which at present are at the head of the accession list (including the Czech Republic[20]) have sizeable agricultural sectors, so even with the first wave of eastward enlargement fundamental questions concerning the size of transfers and mechanisms to adopt have to be decided.

Expected contributions to the EU budget

The Edinburgh summit fixed the ceiling on contributions of the EU member states to the EC budget at 1.27% of GDP. It appears unlikely that there will be the political willingness necessary to increase that ceiling in the next financial perspective which is due to begin after 1999.[21] Part of the ceiling of the 1994-99 package remains unspent[22] and could be reallocated for spending over the 2000-2006 period.

Progress in the accession negotiations depends on the ability of the accession countries to take on the *acquis*. Given the complexity of this task, it is highly unlikely that the five front-runners will join the EU in 2002 (the working hypothesis of the financial perspective set out in Agenda 2000). Any slip in the accession deadline would allow a certain flexibility in reallocating expenditure over the 2000-2006 period.

CEPR (1992) presents the results of a regression analysis which suggest that GDP is a very good predictor of contributions to the EC Budget. Taking the Edinburgh ceiling of 1.27% of GDP as a guide to contributions to the EU budget, and applying this percentage to 1994 levels of GDP in the CEECs, Table 23 and Figure 4 provide a very rough guide to the relative contribution of various CEECs to the EU budget. Clearly, if growth rates differ between the CEECs, their relative contribution to the EU budget after accession will also be affected.

Economic Implications

The impact of enlargement in stages on trade

As a result of the provisions of the Europe Agreements, a free trade area in manufactured products (and to some extent services) will be in place before enlargement, including both the CEECs which join, and those which do not.

The Europe Agreements permit the continued use of "contingent protection", or anti-dumping and safeguard measures[23] in EU-CEEC trade, but at least during the first years of operation of the Europe Agreements the use of these instruments was very limited.[24] The EU has made it clear that it will not consider elimination of its commercial policy instruments until the CEECs have applied the *acquis communautaire* with regard to competition policy and state aids fairly comprehensively.

As Tables 24-26 show, EU-CEEC trade has been growing rapidly, and there has also been a considerable redirection of much CEEC trade from ex-CMEA countries towards trade with the Community. According to the UN/ECE[25], CEEC(6) exports to the EU grew by 130% in dollar terms over the 1989-94 period, increasing their share in extra-EU imports from 2.7% to 4.8%.

It seems likely that trade liberalisation as a result of the Europe Agreements was only one of the factors contributing to the rapid growth in EU-CEEC trade. Over time the pattern of trade growth appears to have reflected the evolution of real exchange rates (Halpern and Wyplosz, 1995) and cyclical changes in Western import demand. A number of studies[26] suggest that the increase in East-West trade represents a return to a more natural trade pattern following removal of the artificial distortions of the central-planning system.

There has also been much debate about how far the increase in EU-CEEC trade resulted from the collapse in the CMEA and the need to redirect trade to Western markets in order to eliminate unsold inventories and huge excess capacities. It has been argued that this may have led to "distress" trade in the sense that the CEECs were forced to sell products which would have been destined to Eastern markets at any price that could be obtained in the EU. This need to find new outlets was exacerbated by domestic recession in the ex-CMEA area during the early years of transition.

Table 27 provides a summary of the scale and speed of tariff liberalisation envisaged for the CEEC(6) over the period covered by the Europe Agreements. As can be seen, the provisions are very similar for all six countries, so apart from minor and temporary distortions which may arise because the provisions for the Visegrad countries came into operation a year earlier, trade diversion between these countries is unlikely to result from the removal of tariffs and quotas.

Full integration into the Single Market and acceptance of the Common Commercial Policy (CCP) have to wait until accession (possibly with the application of a transition period). Enlargement in waves therefore means that different groups of CEECs are likely to move from a free trade area to a customs union (by adopting the CCP) and Single Market at different speeds.[27]

A major difference between a free trade area and a customs union is that the former requires rules of origin. These may be complex to administer and, the regulatory uncertainty to which they give rise means that market access is conditional (Smith et al., 1996). The CEECs joining the EU (and acceding to the CCP and the Single Market) before others will be at an advantage with regard to rules of origin and contingent protection. As a result there could be some trade diversion between CEECs joining the EU and those left out.

This risk could be particularly great as (with the exception of the Baltic states) CEEC exports to the EU tend to be relatively similar. Petroleum and petroleum products, and other raw materials are an important component of the exports of the Baltic states to the EU, and these are generally characterised by a low level of protection in international trade. In contrast, the exports from the other CEECs tend to be concentrated in the sensitive sectors, which are the sectors most subject to protectionist measures on world markets. As Table 28 shows, despite the dramatic growth in trade and the changes in trade arrangements, the composition of CEEC exports has remained relatively stable over time.

A question which arises is whether, as a result of moving to a high position in the EU's hierarchy of trade preferences, the Associated CEECs could displace other third countries in EU imports of sensitive products. Bucher, Hayden and Toledano Laredo (1994) have carried out a detailed study comparing Community imports from the CEECs with those coming from 9 other groups of country.[28] These authors found that the Mediterranean Basin countries[29] were by far the most similar to the CEECs in their exports to the EU. Of the 25 product groups[30] which comprised more than 1% of EC imports from the Mediterranean Basin over the 1990-92 period, 17 also accounted for 1% or more from the CEECs.[31] On the basis of tests of significance carried out on growth rates of EC imports from the CEECs correlated with growth rates of Community imports from 8 other groups of countries for the 1988-92 period, the three authors find a "weak yes" to the question of whether the rapid growth in imports from the CEECs has displaced imports from the Mediterranean Basin.

Table 29 compares changes in the market share of extra-EU imports of the Community from the CEECs and Mediterranean Region over the 1992-94 period. The greatest change appears to have taken place in the category of miscellaneous manufactured goods, but a more disaggregated analysis would be necessary to assess whether, where and when there has been displacement of supplies from the Mediterranean Basin.

The impact of enlargement in stages on agricultural trade

Predictions concerning the impact of enlargement on agriculture are extremely difficult to make given the uncertainties concerning the form of agricultural policy in an enlarged EU. The effect of enlargement on agriculture will depend on the pre-accession strategies adopted, the future form of the CAP, and the way the CAP is applied in the new CEEC members of the EU. The proposals presented in Agenda 2000 offer one vision of how this process will evolve, but, as argued above, it is unlikely that these proposals will be adopted without significant modification.

The EU's pre-accession strategy for agriculture consists essentially of the measures taken to assist agriculture through the PHARE Programme,[32] the agricultural provisions of the Europe Agreements, subsequent improvements in agricultural trade concessions, and the agricultural aspects of the reinforced pre-accession strategy or "Accession Partnership" proposed in Agenda 2000.

The concessions for agriculture of the Europe Agreements were the least generous of those for any sector,[33] and were the subject of much controversy, in particular when the Community's agricultural trade deficit with most of the CEECs was transformed into a surplus (see Table 30). Additional measures which could be taken to meet these criticisms include further improvements in access to EU markets,[34] and increased attempts to ensure that EU export subsidies do not lead to market disturbance in the CEECs.

Agenda 2000 proposed transfers of 0.5 billion ECU per year (rising to 0.6 billion ECU from 2002) to the CEECs prior to accession for the restructuring of agriculture. These transfers could also be used to reduce the discriminatory effect of enlargement in stages on the agriculture of CEECs (temporarily) left out of the EU. The Community already has experience of financing a pre-accession programme of agricultural adjustment in the case of Portugal. A similar programme for the CEECs could be targeted towards the particular difficulties faced by the food industry in those countries, and could help to further environmental objectives and overall programmes of rural development.

It seems likely that CEECs joining the EU will face a transition period for agriculture, but the question remains of what CAP will eventually be extended to the new members. Pressure for further reform of the CAP comes from a variety of directions: the obligations to limit domestic support and export subsidies agreed in the GATT Uruguay Round, the WTO negotiations due to begin in 1999/2000, the new financial perspective of the EU from 1999, and enlargement itself. It appears probable that reform will reflect the shift in emphasis towards rural development and environmental concerns which has emerged since 1988. Agenda 2000 proposes further steps in the direction of the 1992 MacSharry reform,[35] bringing EU support prices closer in line with world agricultural prices, and compensating farmers through direct income payments. Direct income payments (including the compensatory payments) should be used so as to enable rural development and environmental objectives to be furthered. These direct payments would also be at least partially "decoupled" from levels of production.[36]

What then are the implications of extending this altered CAP only to CEECs joining the EU in the first wave(s)? At present prices for agricultural products at the farm gate are higher in the EU than in the CEECs.[37] Though the adoption of CAP-like price support measures and improvements in quality in the CEECs on the one hand, and reductions in EU support prices on the other, can be expected to narrow this gap, it seems likely that some difference will remain at the time of the first eastward enlargement. The higher prices in CEECs joining the EU will act as an incentive to increase production and reduce consumption, thereby adding to the supply balance of those CEECs.

Up until 1992 (and in some cases 1993 or 1994), the significant falls in agricultural production and labour force of the CEECs appeared to render the problem of extending the CAP to the CEECs less acute. However, in 1995 there was a turn-around, with grain production in these countries increasing and livestock production levelling out.

Various of the factors (such as the elimination of subsidies or drought in 1991 and 1992, and in some cases also in 1993) which contributed to the dramatic fall in CEEC agricultural production in the first years of transition were of a temporary or one-off nature. Other aspects of transition, including the fragmentation of farms as a result of privatisation, uncertainty regarding property rights and the high cost of credit, could have more protracted negative influence on production. However, it seems probable that when CEEC farmers have weathered the transition process, output will recover in response to improvements in productivity and price increases.

Tangermann (1993) has indicated various possible causes of productivity improvements: better incentive structures as private initiative replaces state and collective farms; improved resource allocation with the removal of central planning; improved technology; better availability of inputs and capital goods; more appropriate feeding practices; better genetic varieties and breeds; and reduced waste and losses.

The increased income in the CEECs is also likely to lead to some recovery of demand, but it is unlikely that pre-transition levels of consumption will be reached. In the central-planning system the figures for food consumption were probably inflated by hoarding in the face of shortages and wastage, as a result of the poor quality of many products.

The recovery of production together with the higher price levels resulting from eventual extension of the CAP to the CEECs joining the EU could lead to an increase in the net agricultural export potential of these countries. According to the EC Commission's "Agricultural Strategy Paper", this increase is likely to be greatest for cereals. In the long run, the net export supply potential for daily products may be lower, while supply and demand for meat in the CEECs could be roughly in balance.

There has been considerable debate about how far (or whether) direct income payments should be extended to farmers in CEECs joining the EU. At least initially the payments were introduced as compensation for the loss of income resulting from the reductions in price support implied by the MacSharry reform. As the Commission's Agricultural Strategy Paper and Agenda 2000 argue, farmers in CEECs will not experience price cuts, and the application these payments only to farmers could increase income disparities (*inter alia* favouring those who have already benefitted from restitution programmes) and create social unrest. There would therefore seem a case for using at least part of the money available for compensatory payments on more general rural development programmes. A further difficulty arises from the possible renationalisation of the CAP, with the member states paying for a growing share of direct income subsidies. Given the severe budget constraints in the CEECs this could imply less funds available for agriculture than in existing EU members. However, even partial extension of these direct income payments to farmers in CEECs joining the EU would place them at an advantage *vis-à-vis* farmers in CEECs left out of the first wave(s) of enlargement.

Though the exact amounts will depend on the future form of the CAP and transitional arrangements agreed, the CEECs joining the EU will receive relatively large net transfers for agriculture from the EU budget. Ultimately CEECs joining the EU will also benefit from what remains of the Community's system of export subsidies, though the GATT/WTO limits on subsidised agricultural exports could act as a binding constraint on an enlarged EU.[38] This is likely to give them an advantage in competing with farmers from CEECs outside the EU on the markets of third countries and on the markets of the CEECs left out of the first wave(s) of enlargement.

The possibility that firms remaining outside the
EU lose their relative competitiveness

At least from the point of view of moving from a free trade association to inclusion in the Single Market, the Eastern enlargement is similar to that of 1995. One of the main arguments advanced in favour of the EFTA countries forming the European Economic Area (EEA) or joining the EU itself was the loss in relative competitiveness that their firms would experience if they were left out of the Single Market. The creation of a wider, less fragmented market as a result of the 1992 Programme would reduce costs and prices in the EU (12).[39] As a result, producers in countries excluded from this process would find it harder to compete not only on the EU market, but also on their own domestic market and in third countries.

In the case of the CEECs the question of expected benefits from participating in the internal market is rendered more complex, as account also has to be taken of their ability to cope with competitive pressures and market forces (see Chapter 2). None the less, it does seem likely that CEECs participating in the internal market will benefit from an additional stimulus to competition and technical progress, and from the greater scope for exploiting economies of scale.

The way in which the Single Market Programme was presented initially in the 1985 Cockfield White Paper and Single European Act represented a major marketing success. The timetable set out deadlines which fixed precise targets, and focused the attention of politicians and businessmen. At least in the late 1980s, the predictions of an improved economic climate with scope for restructuring of EU industry appeared to become a self-fulfilling prophesy. Would it be possible to repeat this earlier success with the announcement of a clearly-defined, precise strategy for enlargement? The style of the 1995 White Paper suggests that it was an attempted step in this direction.

Although the CEECs will only fully participate in the Single Market after accession, this does not imply that they will not benefit from possible positive effects before then. Integration is an ongoing process and many of the benefits (or drawbacks) will be felt as CEEC policies are aligned to those of the EU. Moreover, Italianer (1995) has shown how much of the reaction to the Single Market Programme in the EU (12) occurred after the policy was announced, and formalised in the Single European Act, and before the 1992 deadline. Similarly, the formal announcement of enlargement could have a positive impact on expectations in the CEECs concerned.

The impact of enlargement in stages on foreign direct investment in the CEECs

Given the scarcity of domestic sources of capital in the CEECs, foreign direct investment (FDI) can play a key role in determining progress in economic transformation. During the early years of transition, inflows of FDI into the CEECs were small and sluggish, but subsequently, as Table 31 shows, they have accelerated sharply. According to World Bank estimates,[40] FDI inflows to the CEECs and former Soviet Republics nearly doubled in 1995, reaching 5% of world inflows compared with only 1% in 1991.

The EU accounts for about three quarters of the FDI stock in Hungary and Bulgaria, two-thirds in the Czech Republic, Poland, Slovakia and Slovenia and just over 50% of the FDI stock in the Baltic States (World Bank, 1996). Inflows of FDI to the CEECs have been heavily concentrated in three countries: Hungary, Poland and the Czech Republic, confirming that FDI is highly selective with regard to location.

FDI may make an important contribution to the transition process in a number of ways. FDI generally involves a transfer of technology, management techniques and of marketing skills. Other firms in the CEECs may imitate these new techniques enabling them to percolate through the economy.

The motives for FDI in the CEECs include the chance to expand into new Eastern markets, the opportunities offered by privatisation, and the possibility of exploiting low production costs. Foreign investors are attracted by the relatively cheap, well-educated labour supply and the nearness of some CEECs to major West European markets. However, the overall economic outlook, the institutional structure and the degree of economic and political stability also play a role in FDI decisions. Economic recovery was one of the factors contributing to the rapid increase in FDI since 1995.

Participation in the programme of regulatory alignment set out in the 1995 White Paper, and an announcement by the EU that accession of a particular CEEC was acceptable can therefore play an important role in influencing FDI decisions. The White Paper sets out the steps necessary for progressive adoption of the internal market legislation on issues such as intellectual property, company law, financial services, competition law etc. In this way it provides a guideline of how to create an institutional framework capable of protecting the interests of foreign investors. The announcement that a CEEC is ready to join the EU is likely to be interpreted as a sign of its progress in transition, and may have a positive effect on expectations concerning the future economic performance of that country. The prospect of EU membership may be seen as a guarantee of economic and political stability, and so reassure foreign investors.

It therefore seems probable that enlargement in stages could lead to a redirection of FDI flows towards CEECs joining the EU at the expense of those left out. The tendency of FDI to concentrate in CEECs marked out to join the EU is likely to be reinforced by the high share of FDI flows coming from the EU and the fact most FDI is already attracted by three of the countries which currently seem to top the accession list.

Against this it might be argued that CEECs remaining outside the EU are at an advantage in attracting FDI because of the opportunities to exploit social and/or environmental dumping.[41] Producers within the

EU might set up joint ventures or other forms of cooperation with CEEC firms in order to take advantage of such "offshore" conditions. However, the 1995 White Paper specifically calls for regulatory alignment in the field of environmental and social policies, so, insofar as legislative approximation proceeds, there should be less scope for this type of "offshore" activity in CEECs outside the EU.

Baldwin, Forslid and Haarland (1996) illustrate how integration may lead to what they call investment creation and investment diversion. Investment creation refers to the incentives to increase investment within the integrating region, while investment diversion entails the negative effects of integration on investments outside the region.

The three authors provide empirical evidence for the effects of the Single Market Programme on investments in the EFTA countries and Spain and Portugal, though they warn about the difficulty of interpreting this evidence. This is partly because the investment decision is strongly procyclical, so it may be difficult to distinguish cases of investment creation or diversion from the consequences of asynchronous business cycles. Moreover, expectations play an important role in influencing investment decisions, so the response in investment may occur following the announcement of a policy, and before the measure is actually implemented.

None the less, as Figure 5 in the appendix (which is taken from Baldwin et al., 1996) illustrates, the evidence suggests that the announcement of the 1992 Programme caused FDI creation in Spain and Portugal, and, at least initially, investment diversion in the EFTA countries. The Cockfield White Paper presenting the Programme was published in 1985, and the Single European Act setting out its formal implementation was ratified in 1987. Negotiations for EU membership of Spain and Portugal began in 1980, and were concluded in 1986. Both countries expected to participate in the Single Market Programme and experienced above average FDI inflows in the late 1980s and early 1990s.

Most EFTA countries suffered a decline in their FDI in the late 1980s, but, with the exception of Switzerland, this was halted, possibly as a result of policies being announced to ensure their participation in the 1992 Programme.[42] As Baldwin, Forslid and Haaland (1996) argue, the different policy response of the EFTA countries may help to explain the different trends in their FDI. Switzerland is the only West European country not to have access to the Single Market, and there appears to have been investment diversion. Austria applied for membership in 1989, and the optimism over a favourable outcome was probably reflected in less uncertainty concerning the threat of the Single Market. After a sharp fall, Swedish FDI began to increase from 1990, and the Swedish application for EU membership in mid-1991 may have contributed to this change.

The impact of enlargement on growth

Baldwin (1989) has illustrated how integration may contribute to growth in both the medium- and long-term. According to Baldwin, the medium-term "bonus" is the result of the improved allocation of resources following removal of the barriers.[43] The increase in efficiency will encourage investment, but eventually this higher than normal rate of investment will disappear. With the increased level of capital formation, the capital to labour ratio rises, and the incentive to invest in more capital diminishes and eventually peters out.

Baldwin draws on endogenous growth theory as developed by Romer (1986) to illustrate how trade liberalisation may lead to a long-term growth effect. Continual growth of output per person in the long run requires ceaseless accumulation of factors of production. In order to endogenize growth it is necessary to endogenize investment. The decision to accumulate factors of production will depend on the costs and benefits of investment. Continual accumulation therefore requires that the return on investment does not fall as capital stock rises.[44]

Various explanations of how this may occur have been advanced. Much of the literature relies on the concept of productivity-boosting knowledge capital. For example, a firm may invest in knowledge to increase its advantage *vis-à-vis* other firms. The additional profits from exploiting this knowledge represent the return on investment in knowledge capital for the firm. However, the investment will have a spillover effect in increasing the stock of knowledge in the economy. It is assumed that this spillover will increase the productivity of resources used in innovating.

The model developed by Lucas (1988) focuses on the role played by human capital in contributing to growth.[45] Individuals will invest in skills because they expect that there will be adequate capital for their higher skills to be reflected in higher salaries. Firms invest in capital as they anticipate that there will be sufficient skilled workers for the firm to earn a profit. There is a positive spillover as those investing in human capital do not consider the output-boosting effect that their investment will have.

The next question which arises concerns how integration may contribute to long-term growth. The elimination of barriers may facilitate international flows of knowledge. This could reduce the cost of innovation, thereby increasing the private return on R&D and encouraging more resources to be drawn into innovation. At the same time the creation of a larger market could increase the profitability of innovation.

In the case of the CEECs integration can contribute to the transfer of knowledge in a number of ways. As shown above, FDI, which is encouraged by the liberalisation of trade and capital movements and by eventual EU accession, may play a crucial role. Regulatory alignment, in particular, in the area of intellectual property rights, which was required by the 1995 White Paper may also prove important. Western assistance through the PHARE programme, with measures such as the European Training Foundation, may facilitate international flows of knowledge. However, there is a risk that enlargement in stages could result in unequal development with regard to knowledge transfer.

Integration could also have a positive effect on financial markets, thereby leading to higher levels of investment and long term growth. In particular, greater competition might encourage more efficiency in financial markets, enabling a reduction in the spread between the return earned by savers, and the costs of funds to investors (Baldwin, 1994). The 1995 White Paper on preparation for inclusion in the internal market has given priority to putting basic legislation with regard to the financial services sector into place in the CEECs, and EU assistance through the PHARE Programme is available for this purpose. One of the aims of the pre-accession strategy should be to ensure that CEECs left out of the first wave of enlargement do not fall behind in the development of their financial markets.

Possible implications of enlargement in stages for the location of industry

One of the main risks of enlargement in stages is that it may lead to a geographically divided pattern of development, with the economic performance of CEECs left out of the enlargement process lagging behind, if not deteriorating in absolute terms. By attaching importance to spacial, or geographical aspects, the "new economic geography" approach developed by Krugman and Venables[46] offers a useful framework for analysing why such polarised development might emerge.

The Krugman-Venables approach involves a kind of circular causality. The possibility of exploiting scale economies is an incitement to the concentration of industry, while trade costs[47] are reduced if firms locate close to large markets. Where firms are concentrated there will be large markets and large markets provide an incentive for firms to locate. The combination of opportunity to exploit economies of scale and reduce transport costs makes for this circular causality.

The approach also attaches importance to the fact that location decisions are very expensive to reverse, so expectations play a crucial role. As a result, in deciding where to locate, future policy (or uncertainty about future policy) may be as important as current policy. In a world of multiple equilibria where various outcomes are possible, the credibility of government policy can play a crucial role. By shifting an economy between stable equilibria a small policy change may have large and lasting effects.

According to this approach, factors such as nearness to a large market provide a strong incentive for other firms to locate in that area. This implies that if a CEEC is near to West European development centres, it is likely to have more chance of attracting industry and FDI. In particular, CEECs sharing common borders with the EU (15) may be at an advantage in attracting economic activity, and this effect may be reinforced by linguistic or cultural affinity. As Petrakos (1996) points out, there will be opportunities for transfrontier cooperation in the form of joint ventures, subcontracting, local and regional policy coordination and the expansion of transport and telecommunications infrastructure.

A second likely development suggested by the new economic geography approach is the concentration of economic activity in metropolitan areas such as Warsaw, Budapest and Prague. These cities and their surrounding areas are likely to present advantages with regard to skilled labour, access to (and opportunities for exerting influence on) government offices, the existence of a large urban market, financial services and transport and telecommunications facilities. The economics of clustering, and imperfect information will place small towns and peripheral regions at a disadvantage in attracting industries to locate in their area.

The new economic geography approach emphasises the role that history, accident and expectations may play in the initial decision of a firm to locate in a particular area. As argued above, FDI plays an important part in the transition process. The announcement that enlargement is to take place in waves could cause a concentration of FDI in the capital cities of the CEECs first expected to join the EU, and subsequently that decision would be difficult to reverse. If the decision to leave certain CEECs out of the enlargement process is interpreted as a sign of their greater economic and/or political instability, not only the peripheral regions and small towns, but also the capitals of these countries may lag behind in attracting economic activity.

The literature on the new economic geography also attaches great importance to transportation costs. Only if the transport and telecommunication systems are adequate can industry become footloose. This suggests that by helping to finance infrastructure projects in the CEECs the EU could play an active role in reducing possible negative consequences for CEECs (temporarily) left out of the enlargement process (and for peripheral regions in CEECs joining the EU). There are, however, certain flaws in this argument:

– At present the funds available for infrastructure projects under the structural funds are far greater than those from the PHARE Programme. To avoid exacerbating differences between CEECs joining the EU and those left out of the first wave of enlargement, such difference in treatment will have to be reduced. For this reason Agenda 2000 proposed an intermediate programme between PHARE and EC policies which involves participation of all CEECs in certain cost-intensive EC policies such as structural measures prior to accession.

– As the experience of the Italian Mezzogiorno suggests, the provision of infrastructure is a necessary but not sufficient reason for the development of a region.

– The link between transport costs and the location of industry is not simple and monotonic. There is a risk that improved transport infrastructure enables people to move to where the jobs are faster than the jobs move to people (Petrakos, 1996).

Labour migration

One of the fears in existing EU member states is that with removal of the barriers, large-scale migratory pressures towards the West will emerge. With accession workers in CEECs joining the EU are (eventually) likely to be granted more favourable conditions in searching for jobs in West Europe, than those in CEECs left out of the enlargement process. In order to assess the importance of this advantage, it is necessary consider the possible scale of East-West migration, and its probable effects.

The question of whether (or for how long) freedom of labour movement will be subject to a transitional period after enlargement remains an open question. In the Europe Agreements freedom of movement of people was said to require "phased introduction", though there was a commitment to EC measures to ease the process. A long transition period would help to assuage Western fears concerning migratory pressures, but according to some member states (and notably the UK), it would be unacceptable because it runs counter to one of the fundamental tenets of the Single Market Programme.

The experiences of Albania, ex-Yugoslavia and the GDR prior to unification[48] are sometimes quoted as justification for the fear of mass migration from the East. In these cases the pressure for migration emerged as a result of uncertainty, economic and political collapse and/or ethnic crisis and armed conflict. One of the main aims of the criteria for accession spelled out at the Copenhagen Summit was to avoid prospective EU members sharing these characteristics.

Much of the recent literature suggests that, provided ethnic upheaval and major civil strife can be avoided, migration in an enlarged EU will be on a manageable scale. However, predictions concerning migration are notoriously difficult to make, as a sudden worsening (or improvement) in economic conditions may alter the pressure to migrate substantially. If a hard core of EU members decided to move forward on a faster integration track, pressures to migrate could increase.

Most of the studies of possible East-West migration rely on comparisons with migrations between South and North Europe in the 1950s to 1970s, and with the North American experience. On the basis of such comparisons, the CEPR (1992) study suggests that 5-10% of a given population might be prepared to migrate with wage differences of about 3-to-1. Layard et al. (1992) maintain that East-West migration could amount to some 13 million people over a 15 year period,[49] possibly comprising about 3.3 million ethnic Germans, 4 million from the CEECs and 6 million from the former Soviet Union. These estimates amount to about 3% of the population of origin, and would entail an annual flow of about 0.3% of the West European population.

Faini and Venturini (1994) offer an explanation of why the pressure to migrate may be on a limited scale. Individuals have a preference for living in their own country for social, cultural and linguistic reasons. Migration is an inferior good (and staying at home is the "normal" good) so an individual will only undertake migration when the wage differential is large enough to offset the non-monetary costs of migration.

Migration will also depend on the chances of finding a job, the level of unemployment benefits, the availability of housing, travel costs and information costs. Faini (1995) also argues that *ceteris paribus* countries with a large informal sector tend to be attractive to immigrants because lower skills are generally required for employment. Moreover, aside from border controls, work permits constitute one of the main mechanisms for limiting immigration, and the informal economy represents a means of bypassing this control.

With regard to the effects of migration, in the long run it seems likely that unemployment rates are independent of the size of the labour force. In the short run an increase in exogenous migration will "simply shift unemployment from East to West" (Layard et al. 1992, p. 42). However, as unemployment rises in the West, this puts downward pressure on wages, and eventually Western unemployment will revert to its original level. The difficulty lies in assessing how long this process of adjustment will take.

The costs of migration are lower for younger workers and as these are often the more dynamic and skilled workers, an enlarged EU could benefit from the rejuvenating effect on its labour force. However, the home CEEC could lose just the skilled workers (who have generally been educated at public expense) needed for economic reconstruction. CEECs granted freedom of movement by the EU would benefit from remittances sent home by immigrants. Many of those who emigrate subsequently return home, bringing with them Western know-how. *Ceteris paribus* the outflow of labour from such CEECs (where labour abounds) would raise capital/labour ratios in those countries, thereby increasing incomes. Although liberalisation of trade and capital movements should also tend to equate capital/labour ratios and reduce the incentive to migrate, in practice they are unlikely to prove sufficient to remove that incentive.[50]

As argued above, enlargement in stages could place CEECs left out of the first wave(s) at a disadvantage with regard to foreign investment and the competitiveness of their industry. Insofar as this is reflected in larger wage differentials and a slower recovery of employment, pressures for migration from these countries to an enlarged EU (in particular, among the younger part of the labour force) could increase.

Implications for security and foreign policy

Enlargement to the CEECs could have implications for the EU's "internal" security. The Union might find that it has imported instability, if there are tensions and disputes between those states that join in the same wave, or if the transition generates societal and political instability even after enlargement. In this respect, it should be reiterated that the conditional promise of enlargement is a "consumable power resource": once it has been fulfilled, the EU loses the leverage it may have had to encourage the applicant state to "behave".

Enlargement to the CEECs will inevitably have implications for the EU's relations with outsiders. It will be expensive and absorb EU resources; the EU will probably be even more inward-looking than it has been during the 1990s debates on institutional reform (in the Maastricht Treaty negotiations and ratification process and the 1996-1997 intergovernmental conference). This could mean that external relations/foreign policy is accorded less attention than it is now. The focus of EU foreign policy will also fall much more on relations within Europe, which could entail a change in foreign policy orientation for member states such as the UK and France, whose international concerns have traditionally been much wider.

How difficult it will be to forge a consensus within the Union on foreign policy remains, of course, to be seen. The arrangements for EU-CEEC dialogue on CFSP matters (the "enhanced dialogue", part of the structured relationship) seem to be fairly successful, and the CEECs have aligned themselves with many CFSP statements and common positions.[51] An enlargement in stages would make it easier to absorb and socialize the new member states into the CFSP. But consensus-building is bound to take more time in a larger, more diverse group.

Member states might be tempted to "go it alone" to a greater extent than now.

As already noted in section 1 of Chapter 3, taking decisions in the security/defense field will remain a complicated affair after enlargement, given that the memberships of the EU, WEU, and NATO look set to differ for some time to come. Again, this could lead to a frustration with collective action, and an increasing tendency for states to attempt to act alone (as France has done in Africa) or within a smaller group (such as the Italian-led mission to Albania).

The Union's relations with Russia and the former Soviet republics could be affected by enlargement. Any new member state "imports" into the Community/Union its own foreign policy concerns and international interests. In the case of the CEECs, enlargement will inevitably mean that there will be a larger "lobby" concerned with relations with Russia, in particular. The CEECs (and particularly the Baltic republics) believe that joining Western security organisations (including the EU and WEU) will provide them with security *vis-à-vis* Russia, an indication of the suspicion and even antagonism between the associates and Russia. Once in the EU, the new member states could push for a harder stance against Russia. Current attempts by the EU to strengthen economic and political relations with Russia could be jeopardised.[52] Likewise, EU relations with other "outsiders" in Central and Eastern Europe could also worsen, where there have been problems between them and the acceding CEECs (such as Moldova's with Romania).

There is also the reverse problem: Russia may seek to pressure the EU and the new member states, particularly the Baltic republics. Including one of the Baltic states (namely Estonia) in the first wave of EU enlargement is seen as a way of including them all in the West's "sphere of influence", given that NATO will not embrace them any time soon. Yet Estonia has had serious difficulties with Russia (over, among other issues, its treatment of the Russian minority), and it is not clear how the EU would handle a deterioration in Russian-Estonian relations.

Enlargement in stages will particularly affect relations between the newly expanded Union and those applicant states that have initially been left out. The most stable, prosperous, democratic countries will be allowed to join first, in line with the membership conditions, which means that a negative message would be sent with respect to the associates left out of the first wave.[53] Should economic disparities widen between insiders and outsiders (see section 3 of Chapter 2), it may appear that

EU membership is a likely prospect only in the distant future. In addition, if the EU proceeds with deepening, the outsiders will have that much more to do to "catch up".

Furthermore, the new member states from Central and Eastern Europe, admitted in the first wave of eastern enlargement, could take a tough stance *vis-à-vis* the excluded applicant states. They will be able to influence aid and trade decisions with respect to the other associates, the political dialogue with them, and eventual decisions on future stages of enlargement, possibly to the perceived detriment of the outsiders. This is potentially a problem where relations between the CEECs have already been strained. It will be difficult for a Union which embraces Hungary to reassure Romania and Slovakia that nothing will change after enlargement.

Enlarging first to the most stable countries in Central and Eastern Europe might not help stabilise the other applicants, but rather isolate and alienate them. It is conceivable that nationalist forces in the excluded applicant states become more popular, with negative implications for political stability. The excluded applicants might turn to other countries for support: Slovakia, for example, has signed economic and cooperation agreements with Russia. This risk should not be exaggerated, however, given the state of the Russian economy (and suspicions of Russian intentions), and the pull of the "West" in general.

With successive waves of enlargement seemingly remote, there would be less outside pressure to proceed quickly with painful or controversial reforms. Of course, reform depends substantially on domestic forces anyway, but the loss of EU influence over the disappointed applicant states is a potential side-effect of enlargement in stages. As Kirsty Hughes (1996, p. 6) notes:

> If some countries are possibly looking at a ten to 20 year, or longer, horizon for accession, this - once it is widely recognized in public and political circles - may seriously undermine both direct support for EU accession and any positive and supporting effects of potential EU accession on difficult economic and political reforms.

The consequences of EU enlargement in stages will be magnified by those of NATO enlargement.[54] The combined processes could be perceived by the outsiders as part of a process of re-creating a divided Europe. In July 1997, NATO decided that it will enlarge first to three countries, the Czech Republic, Hungary, and Poland. The division of Europe could thus appear to be an armed one.

While inclusion in one or both organisations would have a stabilising effect, exclusion from both would not. Both the EU and NATO have come under pressure to widen the first stage of enlargement to try to counter the negative consequences for stability. But the attempts by some NATO members to include Romania and Slovenia in the first round of NATO enlargement were unsuccessful. The Commission, however, recommended including Estonia and Slovenia in the first stage of EU enlargement, and several member states have persistently argued that the first stage should include even more CEECs.

There may be a trade-off between applying conditionality and political stability. One solution to the problems of the disappointed applicants would be to leave fewer associates on the outside, even if those countries do not meet the EU's membership conditions. Gabriel Munuera (1994, p. 93) has asked, "What degree of divergence in performance should be tolerated in the interests of regional stability?" But if exceptions to the EU's membership conditions are made for some states but not others, then the legitimacy of those conditions will crumble. And why should governments not wholly committed to democracy and the market economy be granted membership in a "club" based on those foundations? Why should states that are not ready be allowed to join? The dilemma of applying conditionality cannot be fully resolved, but its implications can be managed as discussed in the next chapter.

Notes

1 Balázs (1995), p. 15.
2 On policy networks, see Richardson (1996).
3 Fritz Scharpf (1988, pp. 258-59) distinguishes between these three decision styles: "bargaining", or the appeal to the participants' self-interest and resort to incentives; "confrontation", or appeal to the interests of the dominant actor or coalition and resort to coercion as the ultimate sanction; and "problem solving", or the appeal to common values and resort to exclusion as the ultimate sanction.
4 These issues have been discussed in EC Commission (1992), pp. 14-16, and EC Commission (1996a), pp. 14-18.
5 Kirsty Hughes has warned that a slow and gradual enlargement "could result in relatively slow adjustment within the EU itself (which could result in ad hoc development of inappropriate, ineffective structures)..." Hughes (1996), p. 2.
6 The Amsterdam Treaty provides for closer EU-WEU ties, but not for a merger of the two organisations.

7   NATO has agreed to enlarge first to the Czech Republic, Hungary, and Poland.
8   The term "Structural Funds" refers to transfers made through the European Social Fund, the European Fund for Regional Development and the guidance section of FEOGA (or the European Agricultural Guidance and Guarantee Fund). In addition to the Structural Funds, structural actions also take place through the Cohesion Fund. Introduced as part of the Maastricht package, the Cohesion Fund provides assistance to member states whose GDP per capita is less than 90% of the Community average. The countries receiving assistance through the Cohesion Fund (Greece, Ireland, Portugal and Spain) are obliged to adopt economic policies conducive to convergence. In return they receive financial assistance for projects in favour of the environment, and trans-European networks to improve transport infrastructure.
9   Courchene et al. (1993), p. 114.
10 Their approach is based on the following formula:
    Structural Funds per head = ax (Franco-German GDP per head - GDP per head in the beneficiary country) + bx (Franco-German employment rate - employment rate in the beneficiary country).
    Two estimates of the coefficients a and b are calculated. The first (hypothesis 1) only considers the Structural Funds programmed for Spain and Greece for the 1994-99 period. Ireland (which receives a very high level of spending from the Structural Funds, amounting to 272 per capita in 1992) and Portugal (with its high level of unemployment) were assumed to be special cases and so excluded from the calculations. In the second case (hypothesis 2) all four cohesion countries are taken into account in calculating the coefficients. The coefficients are then applied to the CEECs in order to estimate the additional cost to the Structural Funds if these countries were members in 1995 (see Table 14).
11 Agenda 2000, volume I, p.63.
12 This reallocation of structural spending could be avoided by raising the ceiling on contributions to the EU Budget, but, as explained below, an increase in the ceiling is unlikely to be agreed for the next financial perspective.
13 An average growth rate of 2.5% per year is assumed for the EU(15) and 4% for the CEECs.
14 The main aim of the Structural Funds is to assist the less-developed regions of the EU, and for this purpose 6 objectives were identified, based on the following criteria:
    Objective 1:   the less-well developed areas of the Community, which are defined as those whose GDP per capita is less than 75% of the EU average;
    Objective 2:   regions affected by the decline of traditional industries;
    Objective 3:   combatting long-term unemployment (more than 12 months) and assisting young people (under 25) in search of their first employment;
    Objective 4:   helping workers adjust to technological change;
    Objective 5a: assisting the structural adjustment of agriculture;
    Objective 5b: aid to rural areas; and
    Objective 6:   regions with a low density of population in the extreme North of Finland and Sweden.
15 However, this last proposal may be open to the criticism that it is a way of spreading funds more thinly.
16 See Brenton and Gros (1993) for a more detailed discussion of this issue.

17 Agenda 2000, Vol. 1, Table 2, p.73. These estimates were somewhat modified in the Commission's proposals of March 1998.
18 For an analysis of the role of the farm lobby see *inter alia* Senior Nello (1984, 1997).
19 This approach is hugely oversimplified, in particular, because no account is taken of the impact of extending CAP mechanisms to CEECs on the level of production and consumption of agricultural products in the CEECs. Clearly the more relevant indicators will be these values at the time of accession.
20 The contribution of agriculture in GDP and employment is less in relative terms, but still large in absolute terms.
21 Indeed, the main contributor to the EU Budget, Germany, is questioning whether the ceiling should remain as high as 1.27% for the next financial perspective.
22 In 1997 expenditure is expected to amount to only 1.17% of GDP compared with a financial perspective ceiling of 1.23% of GDP.
23 A safeguard clause in the agreements (Article 24) permits "appropriate measures" to be introduced when a product is being imported in such increased quantities as to cause or threaten to cause serious injury to domestic producers or serious deterioration in the economic situation of a region. In addition there are provisions permitting the introduction of safeguard measures in specific sectors, such as agriculture (Article 15). Although there is a standstill provision in the agreements (no new customs duties or quantitative restrictions can be introduced once the agreement enters into operation), the CEECs may introduce "exceptional measures" in the form of reintroducing or increasing tariffs in situations where there are "infant industries or certain sectors undergoing restructuring or facing serious difficulties" (Article 22). Given the transformation process, most industries in the CEECs fall in to these categories, so the CEECs virtually have a blank cheque to re-introduce restrictions.
24 As Costello and Toledano Laredo (1994) illustrate, anti-dumping cases initiated against the CEECs fell from over 20 per year in the mid-1980s to only 2 cases each in 1992 and 1993. Because EU anti-dumping measures remain in force for 5 years, the CEECs have inherited a number of such measures from their state-trading past. At the end of 1993, 19 such measures remained in force against the CEECs with Poland (6) followed by Romania (5) facing the highest number of anti-dumping actions. In total, only 60 million ECU or 0.32% of EU imports were affected by anti-dumping measures in 1992. The highest share was for Bulgaria (1.24% of all exports to the EC) followed by Romania (0.7%). However, it seems likely that the impact on potential trade, or trade which would take place in the absence of such measures is greater. At least in the early years of operation of the agreements, safeguard measures were rarely used. In 1992, only two safeguard actions were taken: on Community iron and steel imports from Czechoslovakia, and on imports of sour cherries from, *inter alia,* Poland, Hungary, and Turkey (Costello and Toledano Laredo, 1994).
25 Economic Survey for Europe in 1995-1996. These estimates are based on Eurostat data. If, however, as Drábek and Smith (1995) suggest, Germany is excluded to ensure that the statistics are not being distorted by the inclusion of East Germany in German trade statistics from 1991 the increase is still large though less dramatic (64% for Polish exports over the 1989-93 period as compared with 125% including Germany).
26 A substantial literature has emerged concerning the eventual level and structure of EU-CEEC trade. Most of these studies (including Hamilton and Winters (1991),

Wang and Winters (1991), Baldwin (1994) and Faini and Portes (1995)) use gravity models to predict likely levels of EU-CEEC trade in terms of variables such as the income, population, geographical distance apart and preferential trading arrangements of the two partners. A different approach was used by Collins and Rodrik (1991) who use a trade matrix from 1928 to estimate post-transition trade shares of the CEECS and former Soviet Union.

Various authors have calculated indices of revealed comparative advantage (see for instance, Daviddi (1992), Neven (1994)) in an attempt to predict the long-run product composition of CEEC trade. However, a major shortcoming of this type of approach is that calculation of these indices is based on current trade statistics, which still reflect the choices of the central-planning system and the incomplete nature of transformation rather than any real long-term comparative advantage.

27 A free trade area entails the member states removing all barriers on trade between themselves, though they retain the freedom to implement different commercial policies towards third countries. In a customs union the member states remove all barriers on trade between themselves and introduce a common external commercial policy (for instance a common external tariff). A single market is a customs unions which also entails free mobility of factors of production.
28 The CEECs, China, the Mediterranean Basin countries, South-East Asia, intra-EC trade, extra-EC trade, EFTA, the rest of OECD, and the rest of the world.
29 Ceuta-Mellila, Gibraltar, Malta, Turkey, Albania, Yugoslavia, Croatia, Slovenia, Bosnia-Herzegovina, Morocco, Algeria, Tunisia, Libya, Egypt, Cyprus, Lebanon, Syria, Israel, and Jordan.
30 3-digit NACE groups.
31 Among the products were: basic industrial chemicals, electrical goods, textiles, mass-produced footwear, meat fruit and vegetables, and ready-made clothing.
32 Over the 1990-1994 period EU assistance for agriculture and rural development amounted to 578 mio ECU mainly through grants of the PHARE Programme (EC Commission, CSE (95) 607, the "Agricultural Strategy Paper").
33 In most cases the Europe Agreements fixed a quota, rising in time, of EU imports of various agricultural products from the CEECs on which import levies and tariffs are gradually reduced. The concessions were granted on products imported in substantial quantities by the EC from the CEECs during a reference period. For most countries the three years 1988-90 were taken as reference period. Average imports during the reference period were taken as the basic quantity for calculating quotas. In general the concessions entailed a 10% increase in quota each year for the first 5 years, with a levy or tariff reduction of -20%, -40% and -60% in the first three years, subsequently frozen. Tariff and levy concessions granted previously, in particular those under the GSP were to be consolidated.
34 These could include reduced tariffs, increased tariff quotas, and greater flexibility to ensure higher utilization of quotas, and more transparency and prior warning in the use of safeguards.
35 A central element of this reform was a 29% reduction in the target price for cereals and the introduction of direct payments to compensate farmers for their loss of income. In the case of large farmers the compensatory payment was conditional on the set-aside (i.e. leaving idle) of at least 15% of their land, the percentage being reduced subsequently on the basis of the market situation in the EU. The reform package also included measures for other product groups, such as a 15% reduction in intervention prices for beef, and the use of premiums per head of cattle to compensate farmers and to encourage less intensive means of beef production.

36 There has been much debate about what "decoupling" means, and policies vary according to the extent to which they are "decoupled". At one extreme price support is completely coupled to the level of production. At the other extreme, an income bond compensating farmers for a price cut, and also paid to those leaving agriculture would be decoupled, providing no incentive to produce. The MacSharry compensatory payments would be about half way along this spectrum. For cereals they are based on average yield in each region during a historical reference period. The GATT Uruguay Round agreement contains a "green box" whereby agricultural policies which are "decoupled" from production are excluded from the requirement to reduce domestic support. For an interesting proposal which recommends reducing the compensation payments to farmers and increasing payments for environment and cultural landscape, and rural development incentives (thereby further decoupling payments) see Buckwell et al (1997).
37 See Buckwell et al. (1995), p. 43, and Tarditi (1997).
38 The GATT Uruguay Round entailed a commitment to cut export subsidies by 21% in volume and by 36% in expenditure terms for all agricultural products, and it seems probable that the future WTO negotiations will entail further obligations of this kind. The CEECs were bound to zero or very low rates of export subsidies by the GATT Agreement.
39 See Emerson et al (1989), Venables and Smith (1988), and Baldwin (1989).
40 World Investment Report, 1996, p.64.
41 The sui generis nature of transition in East Germany suggests that care should be taken in using it as an analogy in this context. Under pressure from trade unions in both East and West Germany, the eastern Laender took on the West German system of collective bargaining, and wage differentials narrowed rapidly. The sharp increase in GDR wages was not matched by productivity rises, and contributed to the dramatic fall in output and employment. At least in certain sectors the CEECs were at an advantage *vis à vis* East German producers as a result of lower wages.
42 In 1989 Jacques Delors proposed the creation of the European Economic Area and its implementation began from January 1994, but by then Austria, Sweden and Finland had opted for full EU membership and joined in January 1995. Switzerland rejected joining the EEA in a referendum, and Norway voted against EU membership in 1994.
43 Even with a one-off increase in output, if savings and investment stay as constant percentages of output they will rise in absolute terms.
44 As Baldwin points out, this creates a problem since either nobody wants to invest (when the costs exceed the benefits), they want to invest infinite amounts (when the benefits exceed the costs) or they are indifferent to how much they invest (when the costs equal the benefits). To avoid this problem it is necessary for the individual to perceive that the return on his investment diminishes as capital stock rises. This is possible if there is a wedge between private and social returns to investment, and the public (i.e. economy-wide) rate of return is not diminishing as total capital stock increases. Knowledge creation and investment in human capital represent different ways of explaining this "wedge".
45 This could be regarded as a special case of the knowledge capital argument.
46 Krugman and Venables (1990) and Krugman (1991).
47 Trade costs include transport costs, but also the more general costs of adapting to the local market, which depends on information, culture, distance, etc.
48 Following the "fall" of the Berlin Wall in November 1989, immigration from East Germany, reached 340,000 in 1989 and 120,000 in the first two months of 1990

alone. This was a major factor determining the speed of the unification process, and the decision to allow wage rate differentials between East and West Germany to narrow rapidly (in the process rendering much of East German industry uncompetitive).

49 However, the assumptions made by Layard et al. concerning income disparities (10 times higher in West Berlin than in Poznan) appear exaggerated, especially if PPP comparisons are taken into account.

50 See Layard et al. (1992) for a discussion of this issue.

51 The structured relationship provides for regular meetings (once or twice a year) between ministers from the EU and the CEECs in virtually all areas of the Union. Under the provisions of the enhanced dialogue, there are joint meetings at all levels (from heads of state to expert), and the associates can back Troika démarches and CFSP statements, and participate in certain CFSP joint actions.

52 The case of relations between Greece, the Community/Union and Turkey should serve as a warning of what could happen with relations between the EU and Russia.

53 And indeed the publication of the Commission's opinions was greeted with dismay in several CEECs partly for this reason, particularly where progress with reforms had recently been rapid (as in Romania).

54 On the two process, see W. Wallace (1996).

4 Managing Enlargement in Stages

The potential problems outlined above indicate that the process of enlargement in stages must be well managed if it is to be successful, and spread security and prosperity eastward. A key issue is that of the relations between the EU as it is enlarged in the first wave, and the remaining applicant countries. The excluded countries must still perceive EU membership as a real possibility if they meet the Copenhagen European Council conditions. How to achieve this, however, is problematic.

Proposals were repeatedly aired to begin accession negotiations with all of the applicants at the same time, and conduct some of those negotiations at a much slower pace or even put them on hold. This is the so-called "regatta option" (all the "boats" line up at the start together). The advantage of this option is that it would demonstrate the Union's political will to enlarge to all of the associates. However, undertaking negotiations with the ten CEECs (plus Cyprus) would overload the institutions and waste resources. It could slow down all of the negotiations. Clearly, some CEECs will join sooner rather than later, and the regatta option would merely put off the inevitable differentiation among the applicant countries.[1] This option was rejected by the time Agenda 2000 was released.

The EU could also consider excluding the possibility that the new member states can veto the membership applications of the remaining associates. This, however, would violate Article O of the Maastricht Treaty, which states that applications are to be approved unanimously by the Council and ratified by all the contracting states. An explicit or even implicit statement to that effect could at some future point be challenged legally. As such, it might not fully reassure the outsiders. But even if there were to be such an undertaking, the opposition of current member states to a second or third wave of Eastern enlargement could disrupt the

Union's business (either intentionally or as a result of tensions between the member states).

Partial membership might also be one option for handling the excluded CEECs (see Chapter 5). This, however, is generally acknowledged as posing too many problems (as well as being politically difficult).

The Union could instead strengthen the framework for relations with the excluded CEECs. Some of the elements of such a strengthened framework have been indicated in this paper.[2] It could include additional targeted financial transfers, aimed at better preparing the CEECs for eventual EU membership. All of the CEECs could participate to some extent in cost-intensive Community policies such as structural measures, R&D and assistance for agricultural restructuring. Measures could be taken to promote further growth in EC-CEEC trade and to ensure that the concessions granted in the Europe Agreements are exploited more fully. The CEECs should be granted improved market access for their agricultural products. Private foreign direct investment should be actively encouraged and the International Financial Institutions, including the European Investment Bank (EIB), the European Bank for Reconstruction and Development (EBRD, the IMF and the World Bank should continue to support the transition even after the accession of the CEECs to the Union.

Building further ties between the Union and the outside associates, and thus reducing the barriers between them, could help reassure the associates that they were moving "closer" to the Union. The associates already participate in the structured relationship (which includes the enhanced dialogue on CFSP matters) and can apply to participate in EU programmes (in fields such as research and technological development, education, energy, and so on).[3]

But the future of the structured relationship is in doubt, because of dissatisfaction with it. Frequently meetings have been ill-prepared and do not have a specific objective. In Agenda 2000 (Volume II, p. A8/9), the Commission suggested replacing the structured relationship: bilateral relations with each applicant country would be strengthened (through an Accession Partnership), and occasional ad hoc multilateral meetings could be held. The Accession Partnership would be a single framework, bringing together all the resources available for preparing each applicant country for membership. It would include a multi-annual programme for adopting the *acquis* according to an indicative timetable. Assistance would be conditional on meeting the objectives, and an applicant country's membership prospects could significantly improve if much progress had been made. The Luxembourg European Council endorsed the Commission's proposals for Accession Partnerships, which have been set up in 1998. These agreements will be the key feature of the accession process launched with all ten CEECs, and are meant to reassure them that they are still on their way to EU membership.

In addition, a French proposal for a European Conference has been endorsed by the member states. This would bring together heads of state or government (and possibly ministers) to consult on issues that arise in the framework of the CFSP and Justice and Home Affairs (such as the fight against organised crime, and illegal immigration). The first meeting of the European Conference was held in March 1998.[4]

The replacement of a multilateral approach with much strengthened bilateral links (specifically geared towards eventual accession) could reduce the negative implications of exclusion. But an increasing emphasis on bilateralism could give the impression that regional multilateral cooperation is less of a priority, and regional relationships could suffer. The European Conference risks being seen as yet another "talking shop", if it is unable to take decisions.

The advantages of the structured relationship were that it at least introduced the CEECs to the decision-making environment of the EU. Improving it might be a better way to increase the "sense of belonging" to the Union, while keeping the emphasis on multilateralism. Cooperation should take place in pursuit of specific aims, and meetings should be prepared adequately and in co-ordination with the CEECs. Specific aims could include preparation of the CEECs for membership and cooperative projects in areas such as environmental protection, transport, and so on. Furthermore, the excluded CEECs could participate in expert group meetings in specific policy areas.[5]

Notes

1   The Luxembourg European Council decided to arrange a "group photo": the EU is to meet with all ten CEECs in March 1998, to launch the "accession process", but detailed negotiations on entry will only be opened with the five front-runners.
2   For further suggestions regarding the establishment of a "reassurance framework" for the excluded CEECs, see "The EU and Central-East Europe: The Implications of

Enlargement in Stages. Report of the First Meeting of the Working Group on Eastern Enlargement" Robert Schuman Centre Policy Paper No. 97/2 (Florence: European University Institute, 1997).

3   The associates will, however, only be observers in the management committees that run the programmes, if they contribute financially to them.

4   The European Conference was also designed to ensure that Turkey remained on good relations with the EU, following the decisions not to include it in the new pre-accession strategy (although it applied for membership back in 1987) and to open membership talks with the Greek part of Cyprus. Turkey, however, declined the invitation to participate.

5   This would entail building on and extending earlier initiatives. For example, in the economic sphere, the Ministers of Finance of the CEECs participate in the Economic and Financial Affairs Council (Joint Ecofin) and in regular meetings on matters of economic policy (such as those of the Subcommittees on economic issues).

5 How to Grasp Diversity: Institutionalise It?

Enlargement, even in successive waves of small groups of countries, will clearly increase diversity within the Union. To cope with this, the Union may have to devise forms of differentiated integration.[1] This could mean that not only the new member states from Central and Eastern Europe (and perhaps the remaining associates) participate in the Union in different ways, but also that increased "flexibility" would extend to the current member states.

There are several possible forms of differentiated integration:

- **long transitional periods** for the CEECs before full membership;
- a **multi-speed** EU, very similar to the first option, but allowing transitional periods for all the member states;
- **partial membership**, or full participation of the CEECs in only some sectors and policies; and
- a **variable geometry** EU, in which all the member states can choose whether to participate in different policies.

Long transitional periods for the CEECs are undoubtedly necessary in certain areas. Derogations have been very common in the past, and were granted, for example, to Spain and Portugal when they joined the Community. The CEECs would join, either immediately or at a very early stage, the Single Market,[2] the CCP, and the two intergovernmental pillars, CFSP and Justice/Home Affairs. But transition periods (of possibly 5-10 years) will be necessary before the CEECs fully participate in the CAP and might also be introduced for freedom of labour movement.

Full participation in the third stage of EMU also appears to be a long-term prospect for most CEECs.

The concept of long transition periods could be translated and extended to all EU member states. A "multi-speed" EU would entail allowing all the member states (not just the acceding CEECs) time before they sign up for certain policies. It implies that the goal for all member states would be that of membership in all aspects of the Union, but that member states may need time to prepare for such membership.[3] For example, some member states have remained outside of some policies, such as the Exchange Rate Mechanism of the European Monetary System, because they were unable to join. Likewise, full participation in the third stage of EMU will be an option only for those member states that meet the criteria.

Forms of partial membership could also be designed. In April 1991, then Commissioner Frans Andriessen proposed creating an "affiliate membership" category for the Central and East European countries. Affiliate members would have "a seat at the Council table on a par with full members in specified areas, together with appropriate representation in other institutions, such as the Parliament."[4] One of the possible options here would be to allow the CEECs to participate first in the CFSP and the Justice/Home Affairs pillar, and to join the Community pillar once their economies had grown, thus lessening the budgetary burden for the EU. In addition, some observers have suggested extending partial membership in the form of exclusion from certain expensive policies, such as the CAP and structural funds, although this would be politically unacceptable, as noted in section 3 of Chapter 3. Partial membership could potentially be a way to include those CEECs that do not join in the first wave of enlargement, in some sectors or pillars of the EU.[5]

A similar option to partial membership could be extended to all the member states. With "variable geometry", all the member states (not just the acceding CEECs) could sign up to different policies on the basis of preference rather than ability. In other words, the member states could choose voluntarily to remain outside certain policies or cooperation frameworks. There are various precedents for this, both within the framework of the EU (the Social Chapter, the possible UK, Swedish and Danish opt-outs of full participation in the third stage of the EMU, or the Danish opt-out of CFSP decisions that have defense implications) and outside it (the WEU, the Schengen agreement). The Amsterdam

European Council (June 1997) decided that the new Union treaty will allow "flexibility", but under strict conditions: the member states must agree unanimously that more adventurous states can proceed with deeper integration on certain issues.

Numerous difficulties can arise with partial membership and the extension of variable geometry. Partial members could block agreement in those areas in which they participated, in an attempt to receive further benefits or membership in other areas.[6] There is the risk that a "hard core" of member states, having all signed up for the same policies, decide to proceed with even deeper integration, and other member states find that their options of eventually joining the hard core are excluded.

Too much variable geometry and the problem of external representation and the EU's international actor capability will arise in even more extreme fashion than it does now. Achieving consistency between the external economic relations framework (the Community) and the framework for coordinating foreign policy (CFSP) could become even more difficult if there is a proliferation of frameworks and policy areas with different memberships. For example, the procedure for applying sanctions (first a unanimous common position in CFSP, then a decision taken in the Community framework) could be further complicated because of differing memberships in these frameworks.

As Kirsty Hughes (1996, p. 9) notes, "The question is partly one of balance - some variable geometry may enable flexibility within coherent EU structures (avoiding rigidity) while excessive variable geometry may undermine cohesion and the common base of the EU." Helen Wallace and William Wallace (1995, p. 15) warn that "flexibility could erode common interests and undermine collective action." What the core of the Union (in which all member states must participate) consists of would have to be defined, as a minimum requirement for flexibility to function. Furthermore, ways of balancing (voting, resource allocation and budget contribution) rights and obligations would have to be devised.

Some way of incorporating the CEECs, even those that do not join in the first wave, will have to be found that does not destroy the Union or destabilise the European continent. The new member states from Central and Eastern Europe will not be ready to join fully the EU in any event; those CEECs left outside will need to feel that they are still participating in European integration and that full membership of the EU is still a possibility. Given these exigencies, a multi-speed EU for member states, and an intensive multilateral framework for closer relations with the CEECs left outside, might be the most viable option.

Notes

1. On differentiated integration, see Ehlermann (1995); Hughes (1996), pp. 8-10; and Wallace and Wallace (1995).
2. Though derogations on certain issues (for example, relating to some aspects of environmental policies) are likely to prove necessary.
3. See Ehlermann (1995), pp. 5-7.
4. Andriessen (1991).
5. The European Economic Area (EEA) was a sort-of halfway house between full membership and non-membership, although it differs from partial membership in that it does not provide for voting rights for the EFTAns. The EFTAn countries in effect joined the Single Market, but remained unable to participate in the making of decisions in that area. Ultimately, most EFTAns chose instead to join the EU.
6. It should be noted, however, that this could be a problem anyway: the new member states may demand greater financial transfers once they are inside the EU (and the relative voting power of the poorer member states increases). On this, see Baldwin (1994), pp. 182-190 and 202-205.

Appendix

Table 1   Main Features of the Europe Agreements

1. **Free movement of goods and services** leading ultimately to the creation of a free trade area. Timetables would be fixed for reductions in tariffs and quotas, but because the CEECs required time to become more competitive, tariff cuts would be asymmetric, with the Community proceeding more quickly. Exceptions would be based on precise criteria (such as the infant industries argument, or the exigencies of restructuring). Introduction of new taxes, tariffs or other restrictive measures affecting trade (including subsidies) would be prohibited.
2. "Phased" introduction of **free movement of capital and people** with EC measures take to ease the process (such as encouraging the creation of competitive financial sectors by means of technical cooperation, joint ventures and training).
3. The **approximation of laws** in particular relating to company law, company accounts and taxes, financial services, competition, health and safety regulations, consumer protection, the environment, transport and intellectual and commercial property.
4. The **institutionalisation of political dialogue**, with Association Councils to act as fora for decisions and discussion. The Association Councils also discuss matters relating to the agreements, and are supported by Association Committees composed of senior officials. In addition, the agreements provide for Parliamentary Association Committees composed of members of parliament of the associated country and members of the European Parliament.
5. New and closer forms of **economic, scientific and technical cooperation,** including agriculture, industry, research, transport and information systems.
6. **Cultural cooperation** and exchange of information.
7. **EC financial aid and technical support** in fields such as the environment, transport, telecommunications, agriculture, energy, regional development and tourism. Measures would also be taken to assist

Table 1 Continued

small and medium enterprises in CEECs to encourage and protect investment.
8. Common projects to improve infrastructure in particular relating to roads, railways, waterways and gas pipelines.

Table 2   The Fiscal Criteria and Inflation in the CEECs

	Govt. deficit/ surplus % GDP 1995 (i)	Inflation (average annual increase in CPI) Years			External debt 1994 (est.) $ billion	External debt 1994 as % GDP
		'93	'94	'95		
Czech Republic	1.8	21	10	9	10.7	28
Hungary	-5.0	23	19	28	28.0	66
Poland	-2.9	35	32	28	42.2	37
Slovakia	-2.2	23	13	11	4.1	30
Slovenia	0	32	13	18	11.1	15
Bulgaria	-7.0	73	87	63	10.5	100
Romania	-4.3*	256	136	32	5.4	17
Estonia	0.3	90	48	29	0.186	4
Latvia	-2.0	109	36	25	0.364	6
Lithuania	-2.0	409	72	40	0.438	7
Croatia	1.7	n.a	98	2	2.3	15
Albania	n.a	23	10	0.925	45.0	n.a

*1994
n.a Not available
Source: Van den Bempte and Theelen eds. (column i), Eurostat, EBRD, UN/ECE, OECD and World Development Report, Handbook of International Trade and Development Statistics

Figure 1 Inflation in Selected CEECs

(Consumer price index)

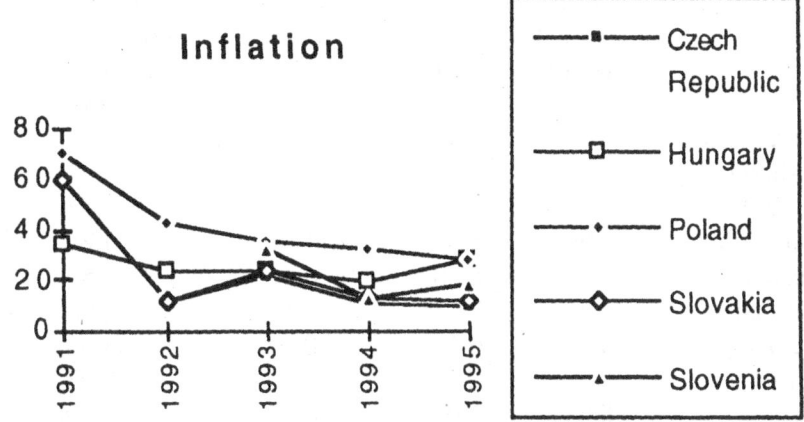

Source: Eurostat and UN/ECE.

Table 3 Interest Rates in Selected CEECs and EU Members

	Long term government bond forecast 1997	yield 1995	Lending rate	Central Bank discount rate (1995)
Maastricht criteria	8.5	n.a	n.a	n.a
Belgium	5.9	7.34	8.42	3.0
Denmark	7.8	8.61	11.8	4.25
Ireland	7.4	8.30	6.56	6.50
Sweden	8.2	9.41*	11.11	7.00
Germany	5.7	6.5	10.94	3.00
Portugal	8.0	10.34	13.80	8.93
Spain	8.0	11.04	10.05	9.00
Italy	8.8	12.21	12.48	9.00
Czech Republic	n.a	n.a	12.80	9.5
Hungary	n.a	n.a	32.6	28.0
Slovakia	n.a	n.a	15.64	9.75
Poland	n.a	n.a	33.5	25.0
Slovenia	n.a	n.a	24.85	10
Latvia	n.a	n.a	34.56	24.0
Croatia	n.a	n.a	20.24	8.5

*1994
n.a Not available/applicable
Source: IFS and EIU (Economist Intelligence Unit) as reported in The Economist of February 22, 1997 for the forecast of long term bond yield.

Table 4   Exchange Rates of CEECs' Currencies

National currency per US$, annual average, official exchange rates

	1992	1993	1994	1995	1996 (Sept.)
Czech Republic koruna	28.8	29.153	28.785	26.451	26.535
Hungary forint	78.988	91.933	108.160	125.681	156.670
Poland zloty	1.3626	1.8115	2.2723	2.4250	2.7781
Slovakia koruna	28.9	30.77	32.045	29.7	30.711
Slovenia tolar	81.29	113.24	128.81	118.52	134.38
Bulgaria lev	24.49	32.71	66.0	70.7	3,201.19
Romania lei	307.97	760.05	1,655.09	2,033.28	12.040
Estonia kroon	12.912	13.223	12.991	11.465	0.552
Latvia lat	0.736	0.675	0.560	0.528	4.000
Lithuania talona	1.773	4.344	3.978	4.000	

Source: Van den Bempte and Theelen eds. (1996) and International Financial Statistics

Table 5 Changes in GDP, Investment and Unemployment in the CEECs

% labour force

	Unemployment rate		Change in total employment	Growth of GDP			Investment annual % change
	'93	est. '94	'90-'94	'93	'94	'95	'95
Czech Republic	3.5	3.2	-9.6	-0.9	2.6	5.9	
Hungary	12.0	10.4	-26.1	-0.8	2.9	1.5	
Poland	16.4	16	-14.9	3.8	5.0	7.0	12.3*
Slovakia	14.4	14.8	-15.4	-4.1	4.8	6.8	19.0
Slovenia	15.5	14.2	-20.5	1.3	5.3	4.1	8.2
Bulgaria	16.4	12.8	-25.7	-2.4	1.4	2.1	14.3
Romania	10.2	10.9	-8.5	1.3	3.9	7.1	
Estonia	5.0	5.1	-18.6	-8.6	2.4	4.3	10.5
Latvia	5.8	6.5	-14.4	-14.9	0.6	-0.8	
Lithuania	3.4	4.5	-12.0	-30.4	0.9	3.0	12.6
Croatia	16.9	17.3	-25.2	-3.7	0.8	1.7	
Albania	22.0	18	-19.4	10.9	7.4	8.9	

* 1994

Source: Eurostat, EBRD, UN/ECE, OECD and World Development Report, Handbook of International Trade and Development Statistics

Table 6 Indicators of the Macroeconomic Performance of the CEECs

	public deficit % GDP (1)	foreign debt % GDP* (2)	inflation (3)	growth of GDP (4)	unemployment (5)**
Czech Republic	+	+	−	+	+
Hungary	−	−	−	−	+
Poland	+	+	−	+	−
Slovakia	+	+	−	+	−
Slovenia	+	+	−	+	−
Bulgaria	−	−	−	−	−
Romania	−	+	−	+	=
Estonia	+	+	−	+	+
Latvia	+	+	−	−	+
Lithuania	+	+	−	+	+
Croatia	+	+	+	−	−
Albania	n.a	+	−	+	−

*Given difficulties in finding comparable data on public debt (the Maastricht criterion), foreign debt has been used here.
** The use of + to indicate an unemployment level lower than the EU average might be somewhat misleading in that a low unemployment rate could be an indication of lack of progress in transition and the fact that much labour remains to be shed.
n.a Not available.

(1) + public deficit less than 3% GDP
    − public deficit more than 3% GDP
(2) + foreign debt less than 60% GDP
    − foreign debt more than 60% GDP
(3) + inflation rates no more than 1.5% above the average of the three countries with the lowest inflation rate in the Community
    − inflation rates more than 1.5% above the average of the three countries with the lowest inflation rate in the Community
(4) + above EU (15) average of 2.4 for 1995
    − lower than EU (15) average
(5) + above EU (15) average 10.9 for 1995
    − lower than EU (15) average

Table 7   The Structure of Production

	GDP million $ 1994	% agriculture '80	% agriculture '94	% industry '80	% industry '94	% services '80	% services '94
Czech Republic	36,024	7	6	63	39	30	55
Hungary	41,374	n.a	7	n.a	33	n.a	60
Poland	92,580	n.a	6	n.a	40	n.a	54
Slovakia	12,370	7	7	63	36	30	57
Slovenia	14,037	n.a	5	n.a	38	n.a	57
Bulgaria	10,199	14	13	54	35	32	53
Romania	30,086	n.a	21	n.a	33	n.a	46
Estonia	4,578	14	10	49	36	37	55
Latvia	5,817	n.a	9	n.a	34	n.a	57
Lithuania	5,224	19	21	53	41	29	38
Croatia	14,017	n.a	13	n.a	25	n.a	62
Albania	1,808	28	55	37	22	35	23

n.a Not available
Source: World Development Report 1996

Table 8 Progress in Transition in the CEECs

	private sector as % GDP mid-1997	Enterprises			Markets and trade			Financial Institutions		Legal reform
	(1)	(2)	(3)	(4)	(5)	(6)	(7)	(8)	(9)	(10)
Czech Republic	75	4	4*	3	3	4*	3	3	3	4
Slovakia	75	4	4*	3	3	4	3	3	3	3
Hungary	75	4	4*	3	3	4*	4	4	3	4
Poland	65	3	4*	3	3	4*	3	3	3	4
Bulgaria	50	3	3	2	3	4	3	3	2	3
Romania	60	3	3	2	3	4	3	3	2	3
Estonia	70	4	4*	3	3	4	3	3	2	4
Latvia	60	3	4	2	3	4	3	3	2	3
Lithuania	70	3	4	2	3	4	3	3	2	3
Slovenia	50	3	4*	3	3	4*	3	3	3	3

Source: ERBD Annual Report 1997
4* indicates standards and performance typical of advanced industrial economies.

(1) **Private sector share of GDP mid-1997**

(2) **Large-scale privatisation**
Four more than 50% state assets privatised; 3 more than 25%; 2 scheme almost ready to be implemented; 1 little done

(3) **Small-scale privatisation**
Four comprehensive well-designed programme implemented; 3 programme implemented, but design or lack of central supervision leaves some issues unresolved; 2 substantial share privatised; 1 little done

(4) **Enterprise restructuring**
Four restructuring programme which substantially improves corporate governance in operation; strong financial discipline at the enterprise level; large conglomerates broken up; 3 structures created to promote corporate governance or strong action to break up conglomerates; 2 moderately tight credit and subsidy policy; weak enforcement of bankruptcy legislation; little action to break up large conglomerates; 1 lax credit and subsidy policies; weakening financial

Table 8 Continued

discipline at enterprise level; few other reforms to promote corporate governance

(5) **Price liberalisation**

Four comprehensive price liberalisation; 3 substantial progress on price liberalisation; 2 price controls remain for some important categories; 1 price controls remain formally controlled by the government

(6) **Trade and foreign exchange system**

Four few import or export quotas; insignificant direct involvement in exports and imports by ministries and state-owned former trading monopolies; almost full current account convertibility at unified exchange rate; no major non-conformity of customs duties; 3 Few import quotas; almost full current account convertibility at unified exchange rate; 2 Few import quotas; almost full current account convertibility in principle but with a foreign exchange regime which is not fully transparent (possibly with multiple exchange rates); 1 widespread import controls or very limited and prudential supervision

(7) **Competition policy**

(8) **Banking reform and interest liberalisation**

Four well functioning banking competition and prudential supervision; 3 substantial progress on banking recapitalisation, bank auditing and establishment of a functioning prudential supervisory system; significant presence of private banks; full interest rate liberalisation with little preferential access to cheap refinancing; 2 interest rates significantly influencing the allocation of credit; 1 little progress beyond establishment of a two-tier system.

(9) **Securities market and non-bank financial institutions**

(10) **Extensiveness and effectiveness of legal rules on investment**

Table 9 The Share of Intra-industry Trade* in EU Trade with the CEECs

	1994	1995		1994	1995
Slovenia	65	68	Albania	28	35
Czech Rep.	61	65	Lithuania	20	34
Hungary	61	60	Estonia	20	34
Slovakia	47	57	Latvia	18	23
Poland	42	48	Malta	61	61
Bulgaria	42	41	Cyprus	35	41
Romania	34	37	Turkey	31	35
Croatia	46	43	Morocco	24	25

Source: Eurostat Statistics in Focus. External Trade 1996, n. 7 and n.13

*Grubel Lloyd intra-industry index = $\dfrac{(X_i+M_i) - |X_i-M_i|}{(X_i+M_i)} \times 100$

The index is calculated using the SITC divisions 00 to 99. Its value varies between 0 (the two countries are specialised in different product categories indicating inter-industry trade) and 100 (the countries are specialised in the same product chapters indicating intra-industry trade).

Table 10 Total Assistance from G-24 Countries to the CEECs, 1/1/1990-31/12/1995

(including Albania, Slovenia and the Baltic States)

	Overall assistance billion ECU	%	of which: grants billion ECU	%
EU Member States	32.6	37.82	9.9	11.48
Of which:				
Germany	14.7	16.98	3.8	4.37
Italy	1.5	1.79	0.6	0.70
France	6.2	7.15	2.3	2.66
UK	0.8	0.97	0.2	0.18
Austria	3.4	3.97	0.8	0.94
EU total (EU+EIB+ECSC +member states)	46.1	53.45	16.8	19.45
EFTA	1.6	1.8	0.7	0.78
Of which: Switzerland	1.0	1.13	0.5	0.59
USA	9.8	11.31	5.6	6.54
Japan	5.0	5.83	1.1	1.23
Canada	1.7	1.99	1.2	1.37
Turkey	0.4	0.49	0.03	0.04
G-24 Total (excluding) IFIs	64.9	75.23	25.4	29.42
G-24 Total (including) IFIs*	86.2	100	25.4	29.42

*International financial institutions

Source: European Commission, G-24 Scoreboard of Assistance Commitments to the CEEC, 1996.

Appendix 93

Table 19 The 1994-99 Financial Perspective

million ECU

Total Community Budget*

1993	1994	1995	1996	1997	1998	1999
69,177	69,944	72,485	75,224	77,989	80,977	84,089

of which:

Structural Funds

1993	1994	1995	1996	1997	1998	1999
19,777	20,135	21,480	22,740	24,026	25,690	27,400

Cohesion Fund

1993	1994	1995	1996	1997	1998	1999
1,500	1,750	2,000	2,250	2,500	2,550	2,600

CAP

1993	1994	1995	1996	1997	1998	1999
35,230	35,095	35,722	36,364	37,023	37,697	38,389

*The other sources of budgetary expenditure are: internal policies, external actions, administration and reserves
Source: EC Commission, DG XIX

Figure 3 Proposed Spending from the EU Budget (1998)

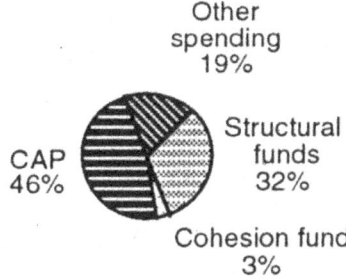

Other spending 19%
Structural funds 32%
CAP 46%
Cohesion fund 3%

Source: EC Commission, DG XIX

Table 20 Extra CAP Spending per Year as a Result of CEEC Accession

Billion ECU

	Visegrad 4	Bulgaria and Romania	Accession of Visegrad, Bulgaria and Romania	1992 MacSharry reform of the CAP included	GATT Uruguay Round Agreement included
CEPR (1992)	2.4	n.a	3.7-7.5	no	no
UK MAFF 1 1994	5.4-13.2	n.a	n.a	yes	no
UK MAFF 2	4.9-14.6	2.6-7.9	n.a	yes	no
Anderson and Tyers (1993)	40.5			yes	no
Brenton and Gross (1993)*	3.7-30.9	1.5-10.9	5.2-41.8 CEEC (6) 4.8-13.4 Baltic states	no	no
Tyres (1993)	22-27	n.a	n.a	yes	no
Baldwin (1994)	11.6	11.6	23.2	no	no
Tangermann and Josling (1994)	13.3	n.a	n.a	yes	yes
EC Commission (1995)#	n.a	n.a	CEEC (10) 12.2	yes	yes
Breuss and Schebeck (1996)	6.8	9.2	n.a	yes	yes
Agenda 2000 (1997)	n.a	n.a	CEEC (10) 11**	yes	yes

Table 20 Continued
*The lower estimates respresent the budgetary estimates of accession with 1992 output, while the higher estimates assume full adjustment of agriculture in 1999
Agricultural Strategy Paper, CSE (95) 607
** Direct payments would amount to 7 billion ECU per year, market support measures (in particular for the dairy sector) would amount to 2.5 billion ECU and accompanying measures would absorb a further 1.5 billion ECU per year (Agenda 2000, Vol. II, p.31).
n.a Not available
Source: Van den Bempte and Theelen eds. (1996) and EC Commission (1994a)

Table 21 Basic Data on Agriculture in the CEECs 1993

	land area (000 sq.km.)	Agricultural GDP $ billion	Agriculture as % GDP	Population in agriculture 1994 million
Bulgaria	111	1.3	10.0	0.9
Czech Rep.	79	2.2	3.3	1.4*
Slovakia	49	0.9	5.8	n.a
Hungary	93	2.8	6.4	1.0
Poland	313	5.5	6.3	6.1
Romania	238	6.3	20.2	3.4
Slovenia	20	0.7	4.9	n.a
Estonia	45	0.6	10.4	1.5
Latvia	65	0.5	10.6	n.a
Lithuania	65	1.1	11.0	n.a
EU	2363	n.a	3	18.1

*Czechoslovakia
n.a Not available
Source: Eurostat, FAO and World Development Report and Tarditi et al. (1995)

Table 22 CEEC Share of Production of Various Agricultural Products in the Enlarged EU total (1994)*

(crop production in 1000 tonnes, and livestock in 1000s)

	cereals %	cattle %	beef and veal %	butter %	dry whole milk %
Bulgaria	3.7	0.9	1.2	0.1	0.1
Czech Republic	3.8	2.7	2.2	4.1	6.5
Hungary	6.8	1.3	0.8	1.0	0.4
Poland	12.3	9.7	5.7	9.5	8.3
Romania	9.9	4.6	4.2	0.8	0.9
Slovakia	2.1	1.2	0.4	0.9	0.5
Slovenia	0.2	0.6	0.5	0.1	0.2
Estonia	1.9	0.6	0.8	1.1	1.7
Latvia	0.5	1.3	0.8	1.8	0.5
Lithuania	1.3	2.1	2.2	3.0	1.3
Albania	0.4	0.7	0.3	0.1	n.a
Croatia	1.5	0.7	0.4	0.1	n.a

*Percentage increase in EU (15) production on the basis of 1994 output levels
n.a Not Available
Source: Own calculations on the basis of FAO data

Table 23 Estimated Relative Contributions to the EU Budget

million $

	Contribution to EU budget*
Czech Republic	450
Hungary	525
Poland	1176
Slovakia	157
Slovenia	178
Bulgaria	127
Romania	382
Estonia	58
Latvia	74
Lithuania	66
Croatia	178
Albania	23

*Estimated at 1.27% of 1994 GDP in US $
Source: Own calculations on the basis of data from the World Development Report 1996.

Figure 4   Estimated Relative Contributions to the EU Budget

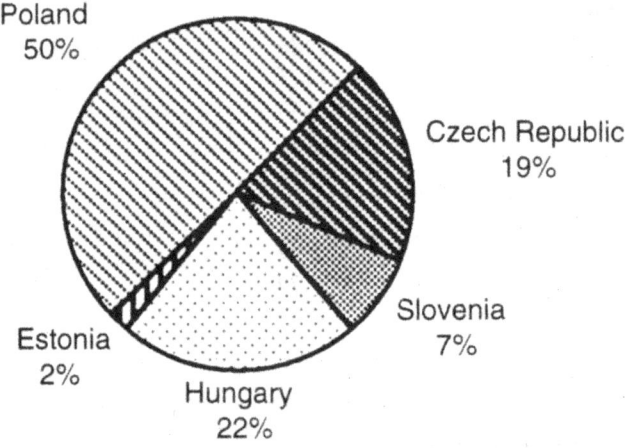

Source: Own calculations on the basis of data from the World Development Report 1996.

Table 24 EU-CEEC Trade

	EU Exports				
	1989 bio ECU	1994 bio ECU	1995 bio ECU	1995 Share %	1994-5 Var. %
Czech Republic	2.39*	7.93	10.12	20.5	27.7
Slovakia	n.a	1.79	2.69	5.5	50.1
Hungary	2.99	6.16	6.77	13.7	10.0
Poland	3.95	10.82	13.50	27.4	24.7
Slovenia	n.a	3.67	4.38	8.9	19.1
Bulgaria	1.5	1.67	1.87	3.8	17.2
Romania	0.69	2.65	3.55	7.2	34.2
Estonia	n.a	0.31	0.45	0.9	46.2
Latvia	n.a	0.49	0.63	1.3	28.8
Lith.	n.a	0.72	0.83	1.7	14.5

	EU Imports					trade balance
	1989 bio ECU	1994 bio ECU	1995 bio ECU	95/94 Var. %	1995 Share %	1995 bio ECU
Czech Republic	2.56*	6.37	7.86	23.5	18.8	2.26
Slovakia	n.a	1.87	2.62	39.6	6.3	0.08
Hungary	2.59	4.96	6.50	31.9	15.6	0.27
Poland	3.86	9.11	11.10	21.9	26.6	2.40
Slovenia	n.a	3.42	3.78	10.6	9.1	0.59
Bulgaria	0.53	1.34	1.76	31.4	4.2	0.11
Romania	2.55	2.51	3.26	30.1	7.8	0.29
Estonia	n.a	0.27	0.43	62.9	1.0	0.02
Latvia	n.a	0.72	0.87	18.0	2.1	-0.24
Lith.	n.a	0.73	0.88	17.5	2.1	-0.05

* Czechoslovakia
n.a Not available
Source: Eurostat

Table 25 The Increase in EU*-CEEC Trade over the 1989-95 Period

	% Increase in EU (12) exports 1989/1995	% Increase in EU (12) imports 1989/1995	% total extra-EU exports 1989	% total extra-EU exports 1995	% total extra-EU imports 1989	% total extra-EU imports 1995
Czech Republic and Slovakia	436.0	309.4	0.6	2.2	0.6	1.8
Hungary	126.4	151.0	0.7	1.2	0.6	1.1
Poland	241.8	187.6	1.0	2.3	0.9	1.9
Bulgaria	25.0	332.1	0.4	0.3	0.1	0.3
Romania	414.5	28.0	0.2	0.6	0.6	0.6

*EU(12)
Source: Eurostat

Table 26 The Increase in the EU Share of the Total Trade of Selected CEECs over the 1989-95 Period

	total exports 1989 %	total exports 1995 %	total imports 1989 %	total imports 1995 %
Czech Republic and Slovakia	18.2 (EC) 4.6 (Austria) 6.6 (GDR)	55.1 (Cz Rep.) 37.4 (Slovakia)	17.8 (EC) 5.5 (Austria) 7.8 (GDR)	56.4 (Cz Rep.) 34.7 (Slovakia)
Hungary	24.8 (EC) 6.4 (Austria) 5.4 (GDR)	63.3	29 (EC) 8.6 (Austria) 6.2 (GDR)	61.6
Poland	31.8 (EC) 0.5 (EFTA)	70.0	34.2 (EC) 0.7 (EFTA)	64.7
Bulgaria	5.5 (EC) 1.5 (EFTA)	37.2	10.3 (EC) 3.9 (EFTA)	38.1
Romania*	28.5 (EC) 3.2 (EFTA)	53.5	13.8 (EC) 1.3 (EFTA)	51.3

* Earlier data is for 1988
Unless otherwise stated the statistics are for EC (12) in 1989 and EU (15) in 1995.
Source: Economist Intelligence Unit (for Hungary, the Czech Republic and Slovakia), own calculations on the basis of PlanEcon and EC Commission, 1994b, (Romania and Bulgaria), own calculations on the basis of Rocznik Statystyczny (Poland).

Table 27 Tariff Reduction Envisaged by the Europe Agreements as Modified by the Copenhagen Summit

	MFN 1992*	GSP 1991#	QR %**				
CSFR	6.8	4.4	22.9				
Hungary	7.5	4.5	25.5				
Poland	6.4	4.0	19.2				
Romania	8.9	6.2	27.9				
Bulgaria	7.2	5.2	32.9				

	1992	1993	1994	1995	1996	1997	1998
CSFR	2.1	:	1.4	0.7	:	0	0
Hungary	2.5	:	1.9	1.2	:	0	0
Poland	2.4	:	1.7	1.1	:	0	0
Romania	:	4.8	:	3.6	2.2	:	0
Bulgaria	:	3.0	2.3	1.6	:	0	:

*MFN duty rate weighted by eight-digit imports within each NACE sector
#GSP duty actually paid
**Quantitative restriction, import coverage ratio 1990
: No change
Source: Costello and Toledano Laredo (1994) and Moebius and Schumacher (1994).

Table 28 Commodity Concentration in Exports to the EU

	Share of the first five commodity groups			first five commodity groups 1994*
	1989	1992	1994	
Czecho-slovakia	34.6	37.1		
Czech Rep.			33.4	electrical machinery (77), iron and steel (67), road vehicles (78), articles of apparel (84), manufacture of metals (69)
Slovakia			42.5	iron and steel (67), articles of apparel (84), textile yarn, fabrics (65), non-metallic mineral manufactures (66), road vehicles (78)
Hungary	39.4	40.0	39.8	articles of apparel (84), medical and pharmaceutical products (54), meat and meat preparations (01), power-generating machinery and equipment (71), iron and steel (67)
Poland	36.4	37.7	43.1	articles of apparel (84), non-ferrous metals (68), furniture (82), road vehicles (78), coal and coke (32)
Slovenia	-	50.2	48.2	road vehicles (78), articles of apparel (84), electrical machinery (77), furniture (82), manufacture of metals (69)
Bulgaria	35.4	39.7	42.3	articles of apparel (84), non-ferrous metals (68), iron and steel (67), footwear (85), textile yarn, fabrics (65)
Romania	70.2	66.9	65.3	articles of apparel (84), furniture (82), footwear (85), iron and steel (67), non-ferrous metals (68)

Table 28 Continued

Estonia	-	58.6	36.5	metalliferous ores and their metal scraps (28), road vehicles (78), petroleum and petroleum products (33), fertilizers (56), non-ferrous metals (68)
Latvia	-	78.4	76.7	petroleum and petroleum products (33), cork and wood (24), articles of apparel (84), metalliferous ores and their metal scraps (28), non-ferrous metals (68)
Lithuania	-	79.2	66.4	petroleum and petroleum products (33), articles of apparel (84), metalliferous ores and their metal scraps (28), fertilizers (56), cork and wood (24)

* two-digit product group codes, SITC Rev.3
Source: UN/ECE, Economic Bulletin for Europe (1996), whose calculations are based on COMTRADE statistics

Table 29 CEEC and Mediterranean Basin Market Shares of Total Extra-EU Imports of the EU(12)

		CEEC			Med. Basin	
Total	1992	1994	1995	1992	1994	1995*
(0-9)	4.6	6.2	7.3	7.9	7.3	7.2
Raw materials						
0-4	1.1	1.2	1.1	4.3	3.6	3.3
Food, beverages and tobacco						
0+1	0.5	0.4	0.4	0.6	0.6	0.6
Crude materials except fuels						
	0.3	0.4	0.5	0.3	0.3	0.3
Mineral fuels						
3	0.3	0.3	0.3	3.4	2.7	2.4
Manufactured products						
5-8	3.4	5.0	6.0	3.1	3.3	3.6
Chemicals						
5	0.3	0.4	0.5	0.3	0.3	0.4
Machinery and transport equipment						
7	0.8	1.3	1.7	0.7	0.7	0.8
Miscellaneous manufactures						
6+8	2.3	3.3	3.8	2.2	2.3	2.4
other	0.1	0.1	0.1	0.4	0.4	0.3

*EU (15)
The Mediterranean Region includes: Malta, Cyprus, Turkey, Morocco, Algeria, Tunisia, Libya, Egypt, Jordan, Syria, Lebanon, Israel, Gaza-Jerico. The CEECs are defined as the Czech Republic, Slovakia, Poland, Hungary, Romania, Bulgaria, Estonia, Latvia, Lithuania, Slovenia, Croatia and Bosnia-Hergovina and the Yugoslav Republic of Macedonia from 1993.
Source: Own calculations on the basis of Eurostat data (SITC 3).

Table 30 CEEC-EU Trade in Agricultural Products

million ECU

	1989	1990	1991	1992	1993	1994
			Exports to EU			
Poland	979	1198	1174	1032	896	959
Hungary	910	867	1089	1005	866	964
Czech Republic	267	286	295	326	271	305
Slovakia	267	286	295	326	52	62
Romania	120	49	90	91	97	119
Bulgaria	160	182	223	214	198	217
CEEC (6)	2436	2582	2871	2668	2380	2626
			Imports			
Poland	826	678	1104	1037	1196	1207
Hungary	151	155	216	299	439	556
Czech Republic	191	174	306	486	483	627
Slovakia	191	174	306	486	131	149
Romania	84	280	260	352	342	203
Bulgaria	112	98	166	142	239	279
CEEC(6)	1364	1385	2052	2316	2830	3021
			Trade balance			
Poland	153	520	70	-5	-300	-248
Hungary	759	712	873	706	426	408
Czech Republic	76	112	-11	-160	-211	-322
Slovakia	76	112	-11	-160	-79	-87
Romania	36	-231	-170	-261	-245	-84
Bulgaria	48	84	57	72	-41	-62
CEEC (6)	1072	1197	879	352	-450	-395

Source: Eurostat

Table 31 FDI Inflows to the CEECs

million of dollars

	FDI Inflows 1994	FDI Inflows 1995	Stock 1995	FDI inflows per capita 1995 ($)	FDI stock as % GDP 1994
Czech Republic	878	2500	5008	242.8	7.0
Hungary	1144	3500	9934	346	15.6
Poland	1875	2510	7389	65.4	5.1
Slovakia	203	250	1140	46.7	7.2
Slovenia	84	130	438	66.8	2.4
Bulgaria	106	135	398	15.4	2.6
Romania	340	373	924	16.3	1.9
Estonia	215	188	646	122.9	10.0
Latvia	215	250	539	97.8	5.0
Lithuania	31	50	103	13.5	1.0
Croatia	98	85	337	18	2.4
Albania	53	70	200	20.3	7.2

Source: World Bank Investment Report 1996 and UN/ECE Economic Survey of Europe in 1995 and 1996.

Figure 5   Net Foreign Direct Investment

Net Foreign Direct Invesment, 1980-1994
negative numbers indicate outflows

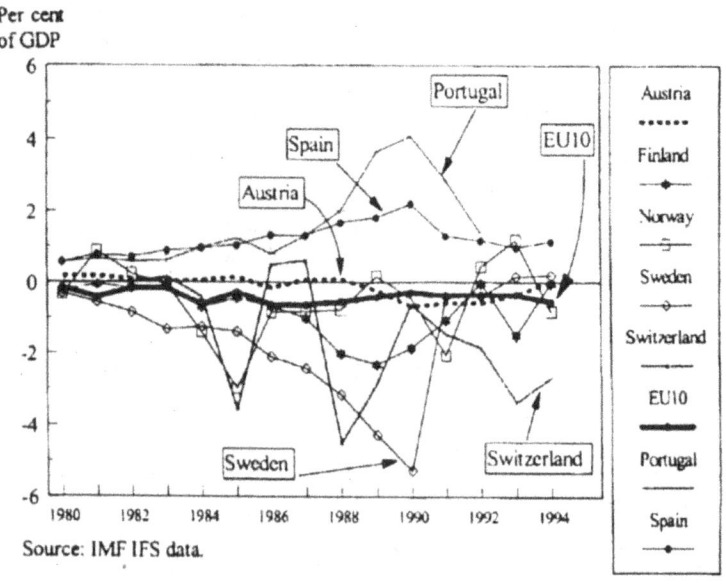

Source: Baldwin 1996

Bibliography

Adameic, J. (1993). *East-Central Europe and the European Community: A Polish Perspective*. RIIA Discussion Paper no. 47. Royal Institute of International Affairs, London.

Altmann, F.L., Andreff, W., and Fink, G. (1996). *Future Expansion of the European Union in Central Europe*. IEF (Research Institute for European Affairs) Working Paper no. 8. University of Economics and Business Administration, Vienna.

Anderson, K. and Tyres, R. (1993). *Implication of EC Expansion for European Agricultural Policies, Trade and Welfare*. CEPR Discussion Paper no. 829. Centre for Economic Policy Research, London.

Andreff, W. (1997). *Nominal, Real, Structural and Institutional Convergence: Is the Convergence of Central Eastern European Countries with the European Union 'Systemic'?* Paper presented at the AISSEC conference, "Convergence and divergence of economic systems", "La Sapienza", Rome, 25-26 September.

Andriessen, F. (1991). "Towards a Community of Twenty-Four". Speech to the 69th Plenary Assembly of Eurochambers, Brussels, 19 April, Rapid Database Speech/91/41.

Balázs, P. (1995). *Strategies for the Eastern Enlargement of the European Union: An Integration Theory Approach*. CORE Working Paper no. 15/1995. Copenhagen Research Project on European Integration, Copenhagen.

Balázs, P. (1997). *The EU's Collective Regional Approach to its Eastern Enlargement: Consequences and Risks*. CORE Working Paper no. 1/1997. Copenhagen Research Project on European Integration, Copenhagen.

Baldwin, R.E. (1989). "The Growth Effects of 1992", *Economic Policy*, vol. 2, pp. 247-281.

Baldwin, R.E. (1994). *Towards an Integrated Europe*. Centre for Economic Policy Research, London.

Baldwin, R.E. Haaparanta, P., and Klander, J. (1995). *Expanding Membership of the European Community*. Cambridge University Press, Cambridge.

Baldwin, R.E., Forslid, R., and Haaland, J.I. (1996). "Investment Creation and Diversion in Europe", *World Economy*, vol. 19, no. 6, November.

Baldwin, R.E., Francois, J.F. and Portes, R. (1997). "The Costs and Benefits of Eastern Enlargement: The Impact on the EU and Central Europe". *Economic Policy April, pp. 127-176.*

Batt, J. (1996). *The New Slovakia: National Identity, Political Integration and the Return to Europe.* Discussion Paper no. 65. Royal Institute of International Affairs, London.

Blejer M. et al. eds (1993). *Eastern Europe in Transition: From Recession to Growth?* World Bank, Washington, DC.

Bliss, C.J. and Braga de Macedo, J., eds (1990). *Unity with Diversity in the European Economy: The Communities Southern Frontier.* Cambridge University Press, Cambridge.

Bofinger, P. (1995). *The Political Economy of the Eastern Enlargement of the EU.* CEPR Discussion Paper no. 1234. Centre for Economic Policy Research, London.

Brenton, P. and Gros, D. (1993). *The Budgetary Implications of EC Enlargement.* CEPS Working Document no. 78, Centre for European Policy Studies, Brussels.

Breuss, F. and Schebeck, F. (1996). "Ostoeffnung und Osterweiterung de EU". *WIFO Monatsberichte*, n.2, Vienna

Bruno, M. (1992) "Stabilisation and Reform in Eastern Europe: A preliminary evaluation", *IMF Working Paper*, 92/30.

Bucher, A. Hayden, M., and Toledano Laredo, E. (1994). "Economic Evaluation of EC-CEEC Trade", in EC Commission (1994b). "The Economic Interpretation between the European Community and Eastern Europe", *European Economy Reports and Studies*, no. 6.

Buckwell, A. et al. (1994). "Feasibility of an Agricultural Strategy to Prepare the Countries of Central and East European Europe for EU Accession", Study prepared for DG-1 of the Commission, Wye, Kent.

Buckwell, A. et al. (1997). "Towards a Common Agricultural and Rural Policy for Europe", *European Economy* no. 5.

Cadot, O. and de Melo, J. (1995). "France and the CEECs: Adjusting to Another Enlargement" in Faini, R. and Portes, R. eds. *European Union Trade with Eastern Europe: Adjustment and Opportunities.* Centre for Economic Policy Research, London.

CEPR (1992). *Is Bigger Better? The Economics of EC Enlargement.* Monitoring European Integration 3. Centre for Economic Policy Research, London.

Collins, S. M. and Rodrik, D. (1991). *Eastern Europe and the Soviet Union in the World Economy.* Institute for International Economics, Washington DC.

Costello, D. and Toledano Laredo, E. (1994). "Trade Access Issue", in EC Commission, "The Economic Interpenetration between the European Community and Eastern Europe", *European Economy Reports and Studies*, no. 6.

Council of Europe (1995). *Human Rights: A Continuing Challenge for the Council of Europe.* Strasbourg.

Courchene, T. et al. (1993). "Stable Money-Sound Finances", *European Economy* no. 53.

Daviddi, R. (1992). "Aiuti occidentali, condizionalità e commercio nell'Europa centro-orientale". *Europa Europe*, pp. 7-30.

Daviddi, R. and Ilzkovitz, F. (1996). *The Eastern Challenge of Enlargement of the European Union: Major Challenges for Macroeconomic Policies and Institu-*

tions of Central and East European countries. Paper presented at the Eleventh Annual Congress of the European Economic Association, August, 21-24.

Drábek, Z. (1995). "IMF and IRBD Policies in the Former Czechoslovakia". *Journal of Comparative Economics* 20, pp 235-264.

Drábek, Z. and Smith, A. (1995). *Trade Performance and Trade Policy in Central and Eastern Europe*. CEPR Discussion Paper no. 1182. Centre for Economic Policy Research, London.

EC Commission (1976). "Opinion on Greek Application for Membership". *Bulletin of the European Communities Supplement 2/76*, Luxembourg.

EC Commission (1978a). "Opinion on Portuguese Application for Membership". *Bulletin of the European Communities Supplement 5/78*, Luxembourg.

EC Commission (1978b). "Opinion on Spain's Application for Membership". *Bulletin of the European Communities Supplement 9/78*, Luxembourg.

EC Commission (1992). "Europe and the Challenge of Enlargement". *Bulletin of the European Communities Supplement 3/92*, Luxembourg.

EC Commission (1994a). "Evaluation of the Cost of Extending the CAP to the CEECs". Unpublished manuscript, August.

EC Commission (1994b). "The Economic Interpenetration between the European Community and Eastern Europe". *European Economy Reports and Studies*, no. 6.

EC Commission (1995a). *Study on Alternatives for the Development of Relations in the Field of Agriculture between the EU and the Associated Countries with a View to Future Accession of these Countries*. Agricultural Strategy Paper, CSE (95) 607, Brussels.

EC Commission (1995b). "Preparation of the Associated Countries of Central and Eastern Europe for Integration into the Internal Market of the Union". COM (95) 163 final, 3 May.

EC Commission (1996a). "Reinforcing Political Union and Preparing for Enlargement". COM (96) 90 final, 28 February.

EC Commission (1996b). "The Improvement in the External Situation of the Central-East European Countries". Supplement A, *Economic Analyses*, 7, July.

EC Commission (1997). Agenda 2000. COM (97) 2000 final, July.

EC Commission Spokesman's Service (1996). "Enlargement: Questions and Answers". Memo/96/78, 30 July.

Economic Commission for Europe (UN/ECE) various years. *Economic Bulletin for Europe*. United Nations, New York.

Economics of Transition (1995). "Selected Economic indicators", vol. 3.

Ehlermann, C-D. (1995). *Increased Differentiation or Stronger Uniformity*. Robert Schuman Centre Working Paper no. 95/21. EUI, Florence.

Emerson, M. et al. (1989). *The Economics of 1992: The EC Commission's Assessment of the Economic Effects of Completing the Single Market*. Oxford University Press, Oxford.

European Bank for Reconstruction and Development (no date). *Political Aspects of the Mandate of the European Bank for Reconstruction and Development*. London.

European Parliament (1996). "Report on the Financing of the Enlargement of the European Union". Rapporteur: Efthymios Christodoulou, A4-0353/96, 5 November.

Faini, R. (1995). "Migration in the Integrated EU", in Baldwin, R., Haaparanta, P., and Klander, J. eds, *Expanding Membership of the European Community*. Cambridge University Press, Cambridge.

Faini, R. and Portes, R. eds (1995). *European Union Trade with Eastern Europe: Adjustment and Opportunities*. Centre for Economic Policy Research, London.

Faini, R. and Venturini, A. (1994). *Migration and Growth: The Experience of Southern Europe*. CEPR Discussion Paper no. 964. Centre for Economic Policy Research, London.

Fayolle, J. (1996) "Rattrapage, convergence, intégration: Quelques enseignements à partir du cas espagnol". In Le Cacheux, J. ed. *Europe La nouvelle vague: Perspectives économiques de l'élargissement*. Presses de Sciences Politiques, Paris

Fayolle, J. and Le Cacheux, J. (1996). "L'intégration des pays d'Europe centrale et orientale a l'Union européenne: un processus à costruire". In Le Cacheux, J. ed. *Europe, La nouvelle vague: Perspectives économiques de l'élargissement*. Presses de Sciences Politiques, Paris.

Gabrisch, H. (1997). "Eastern Enlargement of the European Union: Macroeconomic Effects in New Member States". *Europe-Asia Studies*, Vol.49, No. 4.

Grabbe, H., and Hughes, K. (1998). *Enlarging the EU Eastwards*. Chatham House Paper. The Royal Institute for International Affairs, London.

Halpern, L. (1994). *Comparative Advantage and Likely Trade Patterns of the CEECs*. CEPR Discussion Paper no. 1003. Centre for Economic Policy Research, London.

Halpern, L. and Wyplosz, C. (1995). *The Role of Exchange Rates in the Process of Economic Transformation*. CEPR Discussion Paper no. 1145. Centre for Economic Policy Research, London.

Hamilton, C.B. and Winters, L.A. (1992). "Opening up International Trade with Eastern Europe". *Economic Policy*, no. 14.

Holmes, P., Smith, A., and Young, A.R. (1996). *Regulatory Convergence between the European Union and Central and Eastern Europe*. Unpublished manuscript. University of Sussex, Brighton.

House of Lords (1994). Session 1993-4 10th Report, Select Committee on the European Communities. "The Implications for Agriculture of the Europe Agreements". HMSO, London.

Hughes, K. (1996). *Eastward Enlargement of the EU: EU Strategy and Future Challenges*. RIIA European Programme Working Paper no. 2. Royal Institute for International Affairs, London.

Italianer, A. (1994). "Whither the Gains from European Economic Integration?", *Revue Economique*, vol. 45, no. 3.

Jackson, M. and Swinnen, J. (1994). "A Statistical Analysis of the Current Situation of Agriculture in Central and East European Countries". Report to EU Commission, DG-1, Katholeike Universiteit, Leuven.

Jopp, M. (1994). *The Strategic Implications of European Integration*. Adelphi Paper no. 290. Brassey's, London.

Kaldor, M., and Vejvoda, I. (1977). "Democratization in Central and East European Countries", *International Affairs*, vol 73, no. 1.

Körmendy, I. (1992). "The Hungarian View: An EC Associate's Perspective from Central Europe", in Rummel, R., ed., *Toward Political Union: Planning a Common Foreign and Security Policy in the European Community*. Westview, Boulder.

Kornai, J. (1980). *The Economics of Shortage*. Noth Holland, Amsterdam.

Kornai, J. (1986). "The soft budget constraint". *Kyklos*, vol. 39(1).

Krugman, P. R. (1991). *Geography and Trade*. Leuven University Press, Leuven and The MIT Press, Cambridge, MA.

Krugman, P. R. and Venables, A. (1990). "Integration and the Competitiveness of Peripheral Industry" in C.J. Bliss and J. Braga de Macedo, eds *Unity with Diversity in the European Economy. The Community's Southern Frontier*. Cambridge University Press, Cambridge.

Layard, R., Nickell, S., and Jackman, R. (1991). *Unemployment: Macroeconomic Performance and the Labour Market*. Oxford University Press, Oxford.

Layard, R., Blanchard, O., Dornbusch, R., and Krugman, P. (1992). *East-West Migration: The Alternatives*. MIT Press, Cambridge, MA.

Le Cacheux, J. ed. (1996). *Europe, La nouvelle vague: Perspectives économiques de l'élargissement*. Presses de Sciences Politiques, Paris.

Lucas, R. E. (1988). "On the Mechanics of Economic Development". *Journal of Economic Literature*.

Mádl, F. ed. (1996). *On the State of the EU Integration Process- Enlargement and Institutional Reforms*. Acts of an International ECSA Conference in Budapest, Budapest, 6-10 November.

MAFF (unpublished). *Agricultural Budgetary Implications of Accession by the Countries of Central and Eastern Europe to the EU*. Two draft reports, 1994, London.

Mahé, L., Cordier, H. Guyomard, H., and Roe, T. (1994). "L'agriculture e l'elargissement de la Unione européenne aux pays d'Europe centrale et orientale: transition en vue de l'integration ou integration pour la transition". Study prepared for DG-1 of the Commission, INRA, Rennes.

Martin, S., ed. (1994). *The Construction of Europe: Essays in Honour of Emil Noel*. Kluwer Academic Publishers, Dordrecht, the Netherlands.

Michalski, A. and Wallace, H. (1992). *The European Community: The Challenge of Enlargement*. European Programme Special Paper. Royal Institute of International Affairs, London.

Munuera, G. (1994). *Preventing Armed Conflict in Europe: Lessons from Recent Experience*. Chaillot Paper no. 15/16. Western European Union Institute for Security Studies, Paris.

Nallet, H. and van Stolk, A. (1994). "Relations between the European Union and East European countries in Matters concerning Agriculture and Food Production". Report to the EU Commission.

Neven, D. (1994). *Trade Liberalisation with Eastern Nations. How Sensitive?*. CEPR Discussion Paper no. 1000. CEPR, London.

Nuti, D.M. (1986). "Hidden and Repressed Inflation in Soviet-type Economies: Definitions, Measurement and Stabilisation", *Contributions to Political Economy*, vol. 5, pp. 37-82.

Nuti, D.M. (1994). "The Impact of Systematic Transition on the European Community", in Martin, S. ed. *The Construction of Europe: Essays in Honour of Emil Noel*. Kluwer Academic Publishers Dordrecht, The Netherlands.

Nuttall, S. (1992). *European Political Cooperation*. Clarendon Press, Oxford.

Palankai, T. (1996). "Hungary and Meeting the Membership Criteria - Capacity to Cope with Competitive Pressures and Market Forces with a View to Targeted EU Development". in Mádl, F. ed. *On the State of the EU Integration Process- Enlargement and Institutional Reforms*. Acts of an International ECSA Conference in Budapest, Budapest, 6-10 November.

Petrakos, G.C. (1996). "The Regional Dimension in Central and East European Countries. An Assessment", *East European Economies*, September-October.

Pridham, G. (1994). "The International Dimension of Democratisation: Theory, Practice and Inter-Regional Comparisons", in Pridham, G., Herring, E. and Sanford, G., eds *Building Democracy? The International Dimension of Democratisation in Eastern Europe*. Leicester University Press, London.

Richardson, J. (1996). "Interests, Ideas and Garbage Cans of Primeval Soup", in J. Richardson, ed., *European Union: Power and Policy-Making*. Routledge, London.

Rodrik, D. (1993). "Making Sense of the Soviet Trade Shock in Eastern Europe: A Framework and Some Estimates" in Blejer M. et al. eds *Eastern Europe in Transition: From Recession to Growth?* World Bank, Washington D.C.

Rollo, J. and Smith, A. (1993). "The Political Economy of EC Trade with Eastern Europe: Why So Sensitive?". *Economic Policy*, April.

Romer, P. (1986). "Increasing Returns and Long Run Growth". *Journal of Political Economy*.

Scharpf, F. (1988). "The Joint-Decision Trap: Lessons from German Federalism and European Integration". *Public Administration*, vol. 66, no. 3.

Schumacher, D. and Moebius, U. (1994). "Analysis of Community Trade Barriers Facing Central and Eastern Europe and Impact of the Europe Agreements", in EC Commission, "The Economic Interpenetration between the European Community and Eastern Europe", *European Economy Reports and Studies*, no. 6.

Senior Nello, S. M. (1984). "An Application of Public Choice Theory to the Question of CAP Reform". *European Review of Agricultural Economics*, 11, pp.261-283

Senior Nello, S. M. (1991). *The New Europe: Changing Economic Relations between East and West*. Harvester Wheatsheaf, Hemel Hempstead.

Senior Nello, S. M. (1997). *Applying the New Political Economy Approach to Explain Agricultural Policy Formation in the European Union*. EUI Working Paper, RSC No.97/21, Robert Schuman Centre, Florence, 1997.

Senior Nello, S. M. (forthcoming) "The European Union and Central-East Europe: Background to the Enlargement Question", in *L'Unione européenne face au defi de l'élargissement,* Institut Universitaire International Luxembourg.

Sheehy, J. (1994a). "Foreign Direct Investment in the CEECs". *European Economy.*

Sheehy, J. (1994b). "CEECs' Growth Prospects for GDP and Manufacturing Trade with the EC- A Short Literature Survey". *European Economy.*

Smith, A., Holmes, P., Sedelmeier, U., Smith, E., Wallace, H., and Young, R. (1996). *The European Union and Central and Eastern Europe: Pre-Accession Strategies.* SEI Working Paper no. 15. Sussex European Institute, Brighton.

Smith, K. (1996). *The Making of Foreign Policy in the European Community/Union. The Case of Eastern Europe 1988-95.* Ph.D. thesis. LSE, London.

Smith, K. (forthcoming). *The Making of EU Foreign Policy: The Case of Eastern Europe.* Macmillan, London.

Tangermann, S. (1993). *Aspects of Integration Between Western and Eastern Europe: West Looks East.* Paper presented at the VII EAAE Congress, Stresa, 6-10 September.

Tangermann, S. and Josling, T.E. (1994). *Pre-accession Agricultural Policies for Central Europe and the European Union,* Study prepared for DG-1 of the Commission, Goettingen and Stanford.

Tanzi, V. (1993). "The Budget Deficit in Transition. A Cautionary Note". *IMF Staff Papers,* pp.697-707

Tarditi, S., Marsh, J., and Senior Nello, S.M. (1995). *Agricultural Strategies for the Enlargement of the European Union to Central and Eastern Europe.* Study prepared for DG-1 of the Commission, Siena.

Tarditi, S. (1997). *L'Italia di fronte agli orientamenti della nuova politica agroalimentare comune.* Paper presented at a conference of the Società Italiana di Economia Agraria, Turin, 18-20 September 1997.

Tracy, M. ed. (1994). *East-West Agricultural Trade: The Impact of the Association Agreements.* APS, La Hutte, Belgium.

Tyres, R. (1993). *Economic Reform in Europe and the Soviet Union: Implications for International Food Markets.* IFPRI, Washington D.C.

Uvalic, M. and Vaughan-Whitehead, D. (1997). *Privatization Surprises in Transition Economies.* Edward Elgar, Cheltenham, GB.

Van den Bempt, P. and Theelen, eds, (1996). *From Europe Agreements to Accession.* European Interuniversity Press, Brussels.

Venables, A. and Smith, A. (1988). "Completing the Internal Market in the European Community: Some Industry Simulations". *European Economic Review,* 32, pp. 1501-25.

Walker, J. (1993). "European Regional Organizations and Ethnic Conflict", in Karp, R.C., ed., *Central and Eastern Europe: The Challenge of Transition.* Oxford University Press, Oxford.

Wallace, H. and Wallace, W. (1995). *Flying Together in a Larger and More Diverse European Union.* Working Document 87. Netherlands Scientific Council for Government Policy, The Hague.

Wallace, W. (1996). *Opening the Door: The Enlargement of NATO and the European Union*. Centre for European Reform, London.
Wang, Z.H., and Winters, L. A. (1991).*The Trading Potential of Eastern Europe*. CEPR Discussion Paper no. 610. Centre for Economic Policy Research, London.
Winiecki, J. (1995). "The Applicability of Standard Reform Packages to Eastern Europe". *Journal of Comparative Economics,* 20, pp.347-367.
Zecchini, S. (1995). "The Role of International Financial Institutions in the Transition Process", *Journal of Comparative Economics*, 20, pp.116-138.
Zielinska-Glebocka, A. (1996). "Policy approach towards industrial competitiveness in Poland in the Face of WTO commitments and integration within the European Union", in Mádl, F. ed. *On the State of the EU Integration Process - Enlargement and Institutional Reforms.* Acts of an International ECSA Conference in Budapest, Budapest 6-10 November.

Index

Accession Partnership 41, 66-67
Adameic, J. 29
Agenda 2000 (EC Commission,1997) 2, 5, 24, 36-40, 42-45, 60, 94, 95
Agricultural Strategy Paper (EC Commission,1995) 25, 44, 61, 95
agriculture 37-39, 42-45, 94-96, 106
acquis communautaire 2, 5, 16, 17-19, 28, 33, 39, 40
acquis politique 21
Albania 74, 78, 79, 80, 85, 91, 96, 97, 107
Amsterdam European Council 2, 20-21, 33, 70-71
Amsterdam Treaty 33, 58, 70-71
Anderson, K. and Tyres, R. 92
Andreff, W. 8, 24-25
Andriessen, F. 70, 72
anti-dumping measures 39, 60
Austria
    aid to CEECs 84
    and EC accession 90
    comparative prices 27
    conditions for EU accession 19
    FDI and accession 49, 108
    trade with CEECs 101
    voting rights 88

bad debts 11
Balázs, P. 3, 28, 58
Balcerowicz Plan 26-27
Balkan States 10, 37
Baldwin, R. 34, 49-50, 61, 62, 72, 88, 89, 108
Baldwin, R., Forslid, R. and Haaland, J.I. 48-49

Baltic States 14, 35, 41, 46, 56, 74-107 passim
Batt, J. 28
Belgium
    interest rates 76
    voting rights in Council of Ministers 88
Bofinger, P.13
border disputes 22-24
Brenton, P. and Gros, D. 34-35, 59, 92, 94
Breuss and Schebeck 94
Bruno, M. 9
Bucher, A., Hayden, M. and Toledano Laredo, E 41
Buckwell, A. et al 62
budget deficit 8-9, 74, 79
Bulgaria 1, 8, 9, 22, 26, 28, 36, 46, 60, 74-107 passim

Cadot O. and de Melo, J. 26
Canada 84
capital inflows 16
catching up 9, 34
Cecchini Report 26
Central European Free-Trade Agreement (CEFTA) 23, 28
Central European Initiative (Pentagonale) 28
CEPR, 1992, (Centre for Economic Policy Research) 25, 39, 53, 94
Christodoulou Report of the European Parliament 24
CMEA (Council for Mutual Economic Assistance) or Comecon 8, 10, 12, 24, 25, 40
Cockfield 1995 White Paper 46, 48

Cohesion Fund 35, 59, 92, 93
Collins S.M. and Rodrik, D. 61
Commission of the European Communities and institutional reform 32, 33
Common Agricultural Policy (CAP) 17 25, 37-39, 42-45, 70, 93, 94-95
Common Commercial Policy (CCP) 41, 69
Common Foreign and Security Policy (CFSP) 31, 55-56, 66, 67, 70, 71
concentric circles 2, 3
contingent protection 40, 61
contributions to EU budget 39
Copenhagen criteria 1-2, 5-28 *passim*, 65
Copenhagen 1978 European Council 28
Copenhagen 1993 European Council 1, 3, 19, 28, 102
Costello and Toledano Laredo 61, 102
Council of Europe Framework Convention for the Protection of National Minorities 21
Council of Europe 21, 87
Council of Ministers
    and affiliate membership 70
    veto of new EU members 65
    voting rules 29, 32, 33, 71, 88, 89
Courchene, T. et al 34, 59
Croatia 74, 76, 78, 79, 80, 83, 91, 96, 97, 105, 107
customs union 41, 61
Czech Republic 1, 2, 8, 11, 12, 16, 24, 25, 26, 27, 36, 39, 46, 58, 74-107 passim
Czechoslovakia 10, 26, 60, 85, 99
Cyprus 2, 3, 65, 105

Daviddi, R. 61
Daviddi, R. and Ilzkovitz, F. 8, 15
Delors, J. 3, 62
democracy 1, 19-24, 28, 58, 86
Denmark
    and EC accession 90
    interest rates 76
    voting rights in Council of Ministers 88
Drábek, Z. 25
Drábek, Z. and Smith, A. 26, 60

Economic and Monetary Union (EMU) 6, 15-17, 70
economies of scale 13
The Economist 28
Economist Intelligence Unit 101
EEC Treaty 19
Edinburgh European Council 34, 35, 39
EFTA
    aid to CEECs 84
    and EEA (European Economic Area) 3, 45, 48, 72
    FDI 48, 108
    trade with CEECs 101
Ehlermann, C-D. 72
Emerson, M. et al 26, 62
enterprise restructuring 10-11, 81-82
enhanced dialogue 65
environmental policy 17, 18, 43, 46, 72
Essen European Council 3, 27
Estonia 1, 2, 23, 25, 27, 55, 74-107 passim
ethnic disputes 22-24
EU Budget 33-39, 92, 97, 98
Europe (or Association) Agreements 1, 2, 15, 18, 39-41, 42, 53, 61, 73, 102
European Agricultural Guidance and Guarantee Fund (FEOGA, or EAGGF) 59
European Bank for Reconstruction and Development (EBRD) 11, 21, 66, 74, 78, 81-82, 86
European Central Bank 15-16
European Coal and Steel Community 84
European Conference 67
European Convention on Human Rights 21
European Court of Justice 32
EEA (European Economic Area) 3, 45, 62, 72
European Fund for Regional Development 59
European identity 19
European Investment Bank 66
European Monetary System 26, 70
European Parliament 28, 31, 70
European Report 29
European Social Fund 59

European System of Central Banks 15
exchange rate mechanism (ERM) 7, 70
exchange rates 12, 15-17, 40, 77

Faini R. 54
Faini R. and Portes R. 61
Faini R. and Venturini, A. 54
FAO 95
Fayolle, J. 25
Fayolle, J. and Le Cacheux, J. 34, 92
financial sector reform 11, 14, 50, 81, 82
Finland 19, 62, 88, 90, 108
fiscal criteria 7, 8-9, 74, 79
flexibility of the EU 20, 69
foreign assistance commitments 84, 85 see also PHARE
foreign debt 8, 9, 74, 79
foreign direct investment 13, 15, 46-49, 50, 66, 107, 108
France
    aid to CEECs 84
    emphasis on individual rights 22
    foreign policy orientation 55
    voting rights in Council of Ministers 88
free trade area 39, 41, 61, 73

Gabcikovo dam project 28
Gabrisch, H. 17, 27
GATT/WTO trade negotiations 15, 43, 45, 62, 94
Genscher, H-D. 3
GDR 53, 60-62, 93
Germany
    aid to CEECs 84
    and East German trade 61-62
    comparative prices 27
    contributions to EU Budget 60
    East German wage increases 62
    interest rates 76
    migration and East Germany 53, 63
    voting rights in Council of Ministers 88
Grabbe, H. and Hughes, K. 34
Greece
    and EC accession 28, 90
    and relations with Turkey 63
    and sensitive sectors 12
    and Structural Funds 34, 59, 92
    income per capita 91
    transition period after EU accession 19, 28
    voting rights in Council of Ministers 88
gravity models 61
growth 7, 9-10, 12, 49-50, 78
Grubel-Lloyd index 83
GSP 102

Halpern, L. and Wyplosz, C. 40
Hamilton C.B and Winters L.A. 60
Hughes, K. 57, 58, 71, 72
human rights 1, 19, 20, 21-2, 28
Hungarian Democratic Union Party 23
Hungary 1, 2, 8, 16, 22-23, 24, 25, 26, 27, 28, 36, 47, 58, 60, 74-107 passim

IMF (International Monetary Fund) and macroeconomic stabilisation 16, 26, 66
income per capita in the CEECs 34, 91
inflation 6, 8, 16, 74, 75, 79
    and Croatia 8
    inertial inflation 8
International Court of Justice 23
Intergovernmental Conference (IGC) 33, 55
intra-industry trade 14, 26, 83
interest rates 6, 7, 8, 16, 76
Ireland
    and Structural Funds 59, 92
    EC accession 90
    income per capita 91
    interest rates 76
    voting rights in Council of Ministers 88, 89
Italy
    aid to CEECs 84
    and Structural Funds 52
    interest rates 76
    voting rights in Council of Ministers 88
Italianer, A. 46

Japan 84
Jopp, M. 28
Justice and Home Affairs 30, 69, 70
Kaldor, M. and Vejroda, I. 21
Körmendy, I 29

Kornai, J. 26
Krugman, P. R. 62
Krugman, P. R. and Venables, A. 13, 51, 62

Latvia 1, 23, 27, 74-107 passim
Layard, R. et al 53, 54, 63
Le Cacheux 90, 92
Lisbon 1992 European Council 19
Lithuania 1, 26, 74-107 passim
location of industry 50-52
Lucas, R.E. 49
Luxembourg 88
Luxembourg 1997 European Council 2, 67

Maastricht
  convergence criteria 6-10, 76, 79
  Treaty 6-7, 15, 19, 31, 33, 55, 65
macroeconomic stabilisation programmes 7, 26-27
MacSharry Reform 26, 37, 43, 44, 61-62, 94
Malta 3, 105
Mediterranean countries 41-42, 61, 105
MFN 102
Michalski, A. and Wallace, H. 28
migration 18, 53-55
  and Albania 53
  and East Germany 53, 63
  and ex-Yugoslavia 52
minority rights 1, 20, 21, 22, 86
Moebius and Schumacher 102
Moldova 56
monetary overhang 8
multi-speed Europe 69, 70, 71
Munuera, G. 28, 58

NATO (North Atlantic Treaty Organisation) 33, 56, 57
Netherlands
  voting rights in Council of Ministers 88
Neven, D. 61
Norway
  and EU 62
  FDI 108
Nuti, D. M. 8

Nuttall, S. 28

OECD 74, 78
opinions of the EC Commission 2, 5, 21, 23, 28, 63
outward processing trade 13

Palankai, T. 13, 25
Pact on Stability in Europe 23
Paris Club 25
partial EU membership 69, 70, 71, 72
Petrakos, G.C. 51, 52
PHARE 3, 18, 20, 28, 37, 50, 52
Plan Econ 101
Poland 1, 2, 8, 16, 24, 25, 26, 27, 34, 36, 46, 58, 59, 60, 74-107 passim
policy networks 29
Political Union 20
Portugal
  and sensitive sectors 12
  and Structural Funds 34, 59, 92
  EC accession 19, 43, 48, 90
  FDI and accession 48, 108
  interest rates 76
  transition period after EU accession 19, 69
  voting rights in Council of Ministers 88, 89
pre-accession strategy 1, 3, 35, 37, 66-67, 71-72
presidency of the EU 32
price liberalisation 8, 81, 82
Pridham, G. 28
privatisation 9, 10, 11, 14, 18, 44, 81
production structure 80, 81
public debt 7, 8, 9, 79
purchasing power parities (PPPs) 27, 34, 63

R & D 15
"regatta" option 65
recession in the early years of transition 9-10
regional cooperation arrangements 24, 28
Richardson, J. 58
Rodrik, D. 25
Romania 1, 22, 22-23, 26, 27, 36, 56, 58, 60, 63, 74-107 passim
Romer, P. 49

Russia
    and Slovakia 57
    relations with enlarged EU 56, 63
    Russians in Baltic States 23, 56
rule of law 1, 20, 21, 28
rules of origin 41

safeguard clauses 26, 40, 60
Scharpf, F. 58
Senior Nello, S.M. 25, 60
sensitive sectors 12, 25, 41
Single European Act 46, 48
Single European Market 2, 5, 13, 27, 41, 45-46, 48, 69, 72
Slovakia 1, 22, 23, 25, 27, 28, 34, 36, 46, 57, 74-107 passim
Slovenia 1, 2, 29, 34, 46, 58, 74-107 passim
Smith, A. et al 18, 19, 41
Smith, K.E. 27
social policy 17, 18, 47, 70
Spain
    and structural Funds 59
    EC accession 25, 90
    FDI and accession 48, 108
    interest rates 76
    transition period after EU accession 19, 69
    voting rights in Council of Ministers 88, 89
Structural Funds 17, 34, 35, 36, 37, 59, 70, 93
    and Italy's experience with the Mezzogiorno 52
structured relationship 3, 63, 66
subsidiarity 27
Sweden
    EEA and FDI 49, 108
    EU accession 19, 62, 90
    interest rates 76
    voting rights in Council of Ministers 88
Switzerland
    aid to CEECs 84
    rejection of EEA and FDI 48, 62, 108

Tanzi, V. 9
Tangermann, S. 44
Tangermann, S. and Josling, T. 94
Tarditi, S. 62
Tarditi, S. et al 95
textiles and clothing trade 13, 26, 103-4, 105, 106
transition periods 18, 32, 41, 43, 45, 53, 69-70
Turkey
    aid to CEECs 84
    relations with EU 63, 68
Tyres, R. 94

UN/ECE 25, 26, 40, 74, 75, 78, 103, 104, 107
unemployment 7, 10, 12, 54, 78, 79
UK
    and EC accession 90
    emphasis on individual rights 22
    foreign policy orientation 55
    voting rights in Council of Ministers 88
UK MAFF study 94
Ukraine 29
Uruguay Round (GATT) 43, 45, 62, 94
US 3
USSR 3, 10
Uvalic, M. and Vaughan-Whitehead, D. 25

van den Broek, H. 28
varable geometry 69, 70-71
Venables, A and Smith, A. 62
Visegrad countries 14, 28, 34, 36, 37, 89, 90, 94

Walker, J. 28
Wallace, H. and Wallace, W. 71, 72
Wallace, W. 63
Wang Z.H. and Winters, L.A. 61
Western European Union (WEU) 33, 56, 58
White Paper (1995) 2, 17-19, 27, 47, 50
Winiecki, J. 10
World Bank 46, 66
World Bank Investment Report 107
World Development Report 74, 78, 80, 90, 91, 95, 97, 98
World Trade Organisation (WTO) 43, 45, 62

Yugoslavia
    and migration 53
    and trade disruption 10
Yugoslav Republic of Macedonia 105
Zecchini, S. 11
Zielinska Glebocka, A. 15, 26